E.P. Dutton • New York

nie

A Theatre Memoir by Martin Charnin

Lyricist and Director of the Broadway Musical

Grateful acknowledgment is made to the following for permission to reprint published materials:

Music and lyrics from the musical compositions "Tomorrow" and "Maybe" copyright © 1977 by Edwin H. Morris & Co., A Division of MPL Communications, Inc. and Charles Strouse. International Copyright Secured. Made in U.S.A. All Rights Reserved.

Arf! The Life and Hard Times of Little Orphan Annie 1935-1945 by Harold Gray, Arlington House, New Rochelle, New York. Copyright © 1935, 1936, 1937, 1938, 1939, 1940, 1941, 1942, 1943, 1944, 1945 by the News Syndicate, Co., Inc. All copyrights renewed. All rights reserved. Based on LITTLE ORPHAN ANNIE®, by Permission of *Chicago Tribune-New York News Syndicate, Inc.*

For Sasha and Randy,
who are my children,
and
For Andrea, Danielle, Diana,
Donna, Janine, Robyn,
Shelley, Kathy Jo, and Kim,
who became my children

My father, William Charnin, was a basso-profundo at the Metropolitan Opera for thirty years. He could hit the "c" below low "c," and sing in nine languages, speaking five of them fluently, but in English he sounded like Mel Brooks's 2,000 Year-Old Man. One of his closest friends at the Met was Ezio Pinza, but my purist father never spoke to Pinza again after 1947, when Pinza deserted Grand opera for Broadway.

At matinee performances on 39th Street, I would be tucked away stage left or stage right in the wings and, if memory serves, I never saw an opera from the front until I was in my twenties.

I painted and drew quite well as a child and got into the High School of Music and Art and then into the Cooper Union, where I spent my first two years convinced that Chagall was finished.

In the summer of 1956 a friend and I went to a small resort in the Adirondacks where we waited on tables and worked with the theatre group that was in residence. In our tab version of *Guys and Dolls* I played Benny Southstreet, graduated to the role of the devil in *Damn Yankees*, painted flats for *The Pajama Game*, and went back to the tables during the run of *The Mikado*. But I had been bitten beyond recall. My last semester at Cooper Union was a disaster. I couldn't care less about any paint other than greasepaint.

My father suffered his first heart attack several weeks before my graduation in 1957. The doctors prescribed complete rest, and my mother, sister Rena, and I kept him as sheltered and serene as possible. I didn't quite know how to tell him that in June of 1957, after pretending to be looking for a job in the world of commercial art, I had been dreaming about a career in the theatre and had, in fact, answered an ad that appeared in Lewis Funke's *New York Times* column. The article mentioned Jerome Robbins's forthcoming Broadway musical—a sort of danced version of *Romeo and Juliet*, tentatively titled *Gangway!* —Mr. Robbins still hadn't completed his casting and was auditioning "authentic juvenile delinquents" all day on the stage of the Broadway Theatre. Carrying the one musical number I really knew ("I Wish I Were in Love Again"—an ideal choice of audition material for an untrained singer since it had about six notes in it), I arrived at the theatre along with 2,000 other authentics. It was ten in the morning.

At nine that night, I signed an Actors' Equity contract to play the part of "Big Deal," a member of the Jet Gang. I had made the "Cut" . . . 2,000 were whittled down to 100, and then to 10, and then to me. I sang the song six times . . . I read lines . . . I read four different parts (Big Deal was *not* one of them). I went back to Washington Heights dazed, gloriously happy and terribly troubled. How to tell my father?

My mother and I formed a conspiracy that functioned well for several weeks—I'd get up and go downtown every day and come home and report there were no art jobs available. On days that rehearsals lasted longer than had originally been scheduled, she would tell my father that I was hot on the trail of something. At night, in my room, I rehearsed and memorized in silence, singing "The Jet Song" or "Gee, Officer Krupke" in a whisper.

The month of August presented me with the problem of finally revealing what was going on, since the show (now retitled *West Side Story*) was going to Washington to break in. I confronted the issue on the Saturday night before we were to leave, but had to come up with a buffer, in order to ease the revelation to my father. I took a deep breath and spilled out the facts, mentioning the word Broadway only once, hitting hard on the artistic aspect of the musical and the new ground that it was attempting to break, and then dealing quite slowly with the fact that all of the creators were Jewish—Sondheim, Robbins, Laurents, and best of all, Bernstein. My father smiled. He liked the news about Lenny. He said only one thing to me . . . "You can sing?" And he shook his head and patted my cheek. That night I sang "Krupke" very loudly in my room and my father put on *Boris Godunov* as a rebuttal.

The first afternoon in Washington at the National Theatre that the entire show assembled, Lenny took me aside and showed me a letter my father had written to him. It was pleasant, complimentary to Lenny, but contained a threat—"Take care of my son Martin, or else."

My father had a second attack in September of 1957, while we were out of town, and, when we returned, under doctor's orders, he was not allowed out of the house. He never saw me act, he never heard me sing. He died in 1958 convinced that I would give up the foolishness of the Broadway stage and someday go back to painting. Someday maybe I will.

MARTIN CHARNIN
OCT. 18, 1977 N.Y.C.

OVERTURE:
Maybe

Christmas 1971 was no different than the four previous Christmases had been for me. I was way behind in my shopping, and since *Star Wars* towels and wastepaper baskets were still six years away and the Pet Rock was just a stone on the beach at East Hampton, books were a safe, last-minute solution.

I was in Doubleday's on Fifty-seventh Street and I needed a present for a friend who had some interest in "pop" culture. I bought a book called *Arf! The Life and Hard Times of Little Orphan Annie,* containing ten years of the daily "Little Orphan Annie" comic strip, written and drawn by Harold Gray. Since I was in a hurry I told the clerk not to wrap the book, just put it in a shopping bag.

Come forward, Doubleday clerk, come forward! Had you wrapped the book, I wouldn't have spent the entire night reading it and would never have asked my attorneys to begin negotiations for the acquisition of the rights to the strip to turn it into a Broadway musical. Come forward! You can have house seats for the rest of your natural life!

I look for two ingredients when I start the search for a musical: first, a leading character—someone with substance who can live a life on the stage for two hours, who will have interesting adventures, who has a goal or a mission, who is questing something. The second ingredient is the setting—a place that can be put into a musical frame. Then the trick is to make them gel.

The nature of some comic strips is to put the character in different episodes. In "Little Orphan Annie" the episodes changed every six weeks. Little Orphan Annie was constantly having adventures. She found herself in Hollywood; she was being kidnapped by waterfront characters; she was with Oliver Warbucks; she was in situation after situation throughout the fifty years of the comic strip.

But Harold Gray neglected one minor detail . . . a detail that could become the perfect basis for a musical. Annie came like Venus from the half shell, full-grown into the strip. We had no sense of her origins, nor did we know how Oliver Warbucks and Annie got together. It was that idea I took to my friend Tom Meehan, a writer I had worked with before, suggesting it would be interesting if we could invent it— since it did not exist.

When I called Tom Meehan and invited him to join the project, his initial reaction was comparable to General McAuliffe's during World War II. McAuliffe said, "Nuts." Meehan said, "Ughhh, I hate it!" I know visions of *Pygmalion* (*My Fair Lady*) and of Sholem Aleichem (*Fiddler on the Roof*) danced in his head when I asked him to do a Broadway musical with me.

Tom suggested that the action of our musical take place two weeks prior to Christmas 1933—the first Christmas with Franklin Delano Roosevelt as the President of the United States. We both resisted the idea of doing *Annie* as camp or as a cartoon. We wanted to treat it as a real piece of theatre. We had several lengthy discussions, batting ideas around, and there were two false starts. One was an approach in a much more satirical, comic strip type of way. That version never went past the stage of an outline, for as soon as it was completed, we knew we could never define the characters with any conviction. We could never honor them, because we couldn't believe in them.

Very early, for example, we decided to get rid of the two supernatural characters in the strip, Punjab and the Asp, both of whom were all through Harold Gray, but were stretching *our* reality to the breaking point.

Slowly but surely, we began to focus on the story we had to tell, and the story was twofold:

(1) Where had Annie come from? Where were her parents? (Tom changed her to a foundling. She is not an orphan in the musical; she is left on the stoop of a New York City orphanage.)

(2) The search for Annie's parents had to be woven into the meeting with Warbucks and his coming to love her and his decision to adopt her.

After my first meeting with Tom I told him I had already contacted Charles Strouse about writing the score. Charles and I had known each other during my *West Side Story* and his *Bye Bye Birdie* days, and had often threatened to work with each other, but had never gotten around to it. Charles's first reaction was similar to Tom's—I think there was just one less "h" in his "Ughh!" Charles was no stranger to comic strip musicals, having recently done a musical version of "Superman," after his earlier award-winning musicals *Golden Boy* and *Birdie*. *Superman* wasn't a total success, and his conditioning from that experience, I suppose, was why he believed cartoon musicals wouldn't work. But once we were able to convince him we weren't interested in pursuing Annie on a comic strip level, Charles joined the adventure.

The actual writing of the script didn't begin until the spring of 1972. Tom worked on an outline of the script, and Charles and I worked on an outline of the score. Every few weeks, we would meet to collate our material. Each of us had to make a living, and, while I owned the rights to the musical, there was no producer—therefore no financial subsidy. There was just that private belief the three of us had that Annie would work on the stage. It took sixteen months to write the musical, and when it was finished we made a concerted effort to attract a producer who would commit himself to it. Once involved, the producer could sign a Dramatist Guild contract with the creators, which would pay a minimum amount of money to the three of us. By Guild standards that is $1,500 per author. Amortizing that over the sixteen months we put into it, we would earn less than $100 a month.

Auditioning for a producer is like singing your heart out for Mount Rushmore. The creators assault him with their passion about their project, and the producer is put on the spot. More often than not he responds with stony silence.

The first producer to hear *Annie* was James Nederlander. In 1973, he and his staff were brought up to Charles Strouse's apartment. We had reduced the two-and-a-half-hour musical to a fifty-five-minute demonstration. Nederlander was remarkable. He listened. He laughed. He cried. At the end of the demonstration he simply said, "I like it. I want to do it." He left saying, "Send me the script." So much for Mt. Rushmore.

Nederlander's next communication was a letter saying "thanks for sending me Annie. I haven't read it yet, but plan to get to it on the plane this afternoon. It sounds like a great idea." So much for Mt. Rushmore.

Nederlander had other projects going on then, and our timetable and his didn't allow us to go further. We were very cocky, however. We believed that if Nederlander, who is a reputable, intelligent producer in the business, had said he liked it, then finding another producer would be easy. We were also very impatient. We wanted to begin rehearsals by late summer and be on Broadway in the late fall or early winter. If the producer's calendar was open we could go into production instantly.

A series of auditions were held at the William Morris agency, at Strouse's apartment, and at E.H. Morris and Co., my music publisher. Everyone listened and said things like, "Yes, it's an interesting idea," or worse. Nobody jumped up and down and said, "My God, I've *got* to do that musical!" And 1973 became 1974 . . . and 1974 became 1975. We spent two and a half years without a producer, during which time I had the responsibility for maintaining the rights and paying the legal fees.

Then, in 1975, a gentleman named George Gilbert was brought to us. He had been on Broadway as the producer of *Say Darling* and *Mr. Wonderful* with Sammy Davis, Jr. Gilbert heard *Annie* and loved it. Money changed hands for the first time in late 1974, when Dramatist Guild contracts were signed. Gilbert paid us each $1,500, which meant the amount of money we had made up to that point was no longer $100 a month, but $42.50.

Joseph Cates
presents
Bernadette Peters
as
LITTLE
ORPHAN
ANNIE
A New Musical
Book by
Tom Meehan
Music by Charles Strouse
Lyrics By Martin Charnin

based on characters created by Harold gray

Choreography by Alan Johnson
Musical Direction by Elliot Lawrence
Costumes By Theoni V. Aldredge
Dance music By John Morris

conceived and directed By
MARTIN CHARNIN

Nobody believed. It's as simple as that. We finished writing *Annie* and started auditions. While most of the potential producers were enamored of the score, the concept of the musical was difficult to appreciate. You could hear the songs and like them or not, but at backers' auditions my imitations of F.D.R., or Charles's of The Three Boylan Sisters sounded like pure, unadulterated camp. Camp was the furthest thing from our minds. After four auditions, Tom and Charles and I decided to do a little preamble—stating that we were doing the musical as a *real* story, a *real* story about a child's search for her parents, as well as a love story between her and the fifty-five-year-old man who ultimately adopts her.

The leading role of Annie *had* to be played by a real child. Two agents submitted the idea of Bernadette Peters and Bette Midler with training bras on as potential Annies. But we held fast. Real story. Real kids. No "stars."

No stars equals nothing bankable as far as raising money is concerned. And musicals are wildly expensive. You expect them to cost more than you expected them to cost, but they still cost more than you expected. We kept screaming, "The show is the star! The show is the star!"

There was another problem. I wanted to direct. "Wanted" is mild. I felt I *had* to direct. I couldn't imagine going through this and allowing another viewpoint to come into the project. Risky. One man with two jobs equals no buyers. No takers. No show. But I felt I could not budge.

I dummied up a poster in 1973 after a conversation with an agent about Ms. Peters. Charles hated it and Tom said the next time he saw any artwork his billing should be Thomas Meehan.

ACT I:
It's The Hard-Knock Life

We waited another year, until 1976, when Michael Price heard *Annie* and decided to produce it for The Goodspeed Opera House. Located on the Connecticut River in East Haddam, the theatre is the birthplace of such Broadway successes as *Shenandoah* and *Man of La Mancha*. During the season, which runs from May until October, Goodspeed does three musicals; usually, two are revivals, and the third is an original.

Annie was selected as the third show of the 1976 season. We were preceded by a revival of *Dearest Enemy,* a Rodgers and Hart musical, which was set in revolutionary times and was being revived for the Bicentennial celebration, and by *Going Up,* a 1919 Otto Harbach musical about flyers during World War I.

Goodspeed Landing at East Haddam, Connecticut

Price liked *Annie* but was strenuously opposed to my directing it. His resident director who did the revivals could conceivably do the original, and there was also the possibility of hiring an outside director. I wanted to be the director but was so desperate to get the show on, I took off the director's hat entirely. "I'll be the lyricist, period. I want to see this musical on the stage." It killed me. It was a very painful decision but I made it.

Tom, Charles, and I insisted, however, that if I wasn't going to direct we would have approval of who did. In the early spring we saw three directors suggested by Price. We discussed concepts and attitudes toward *Annie* with them, and all three stumbled over a single conceptual point—they couldn't see the reality in the script

SOMETIMES YOU JUST GOTTA DO THINGS THAT HURT YA DEEP DOWN INSIDE—

—AND HOPE THAT THEY TURN OUT FOR THE BEST, ANNIE!

For the Goodspeed run, the authors receive nothing but the mounting of their show. They get no royalty and, in effect, give the producers—Michael Price and the Goodspeed Opera House —the project. Price and the theatre maintain a financial interest all the way down the line if anything happens to the play after it leaves Goodspeed.

Goodspeed Opera House.

1876

U.P.I.

and each tried to invest the show with an overlay of camp. None of the directors was suitable, and as we got closer and closer to auditions, Price reluctantly offered me the job.

We began to cast the show in May. *Dearest Enemy* and *Going Up* had utilized the resident company at Goodspeed, but *Annie* was cast in New York. Casting calls went out to all the talent agencies, and, during a three-week period, we saw over six hundred people. Of them fifteen came to Goodspeed and eventually ended up in the Broadway company. Reid Shelton was cast as Oliver Warbucks and originally played the part with gray hair; Sandy Faison was his secretary then and now; Robert Fitch, who plays Rooster, Miss Hannigan's ne'er-do-well brother, was in the company, along with Ray Thorne, our F.D.R., Laurie Beechman, Barbara Erwin, Diana Barrows, Danielle Brisebois, Janine Ruane, Edwin Bordo, Edie Cowan, James Hosbein, Richard Ensslen, Donald Craig, and Andrea McArdle.

At the auditions, little girls, six to thirteen years old, all prettied up and beaming like Miss America contestants, paraded in front of us singing songs and doing routines wildly out of character for little girls. We were looking for "unfinished" children—unfinished to the extent that they were not totally complete as performers. If they were super-professional, that is, so molded and styled as some children in the entertainment industry are, I wouldn't be able to shape them from the directorial standpoint, from the book standpoint, from the score standpoint. Some kids come in and dazzle you with their automated brilliance. They do everything too perfectly. We were looking for kids with rough edges and also for specific types: one

Reid, pre-Norelco

Sandy Faison, who auditioned for the role of Grace Farrell six times in six different outfits and with six different accents

Robert Fitch, a veteran of numerous Broadway musicals and an accomplished magician

little dark one . . . one skinny one . . . one chubby one . . . one really tough, street-smart kid. We wanted a mix that was comparable to the gang Jerome Robbins had put together for the Jets in *West Side Story*. In effect, we were making a little gang of orphans. So, each of the kids had to be a very special type.

Andrea McArdle was the second child we saw and the first one hired. She instantly impressed us because she was street-wise beyond belief, super-conscientious, and had a great sense of humor. She also had a wonderful, athletic body. She was tight, built like a gymnast. We decided to cast her in the role of the toughest orphan.

We found another young girl for the part of Annie. She was thirteen years old, small, vulnerable, with a beautiful, beautiful face, and natural red hair—a plus since we would not have to dye it for the role. We put together six children and a company of seventeen adult actors from New York. Some of the kids came from Philadelphia, which we discovered was a good source for young performers.

I foolishly thought that finding a dog to play Sandy would be easy, but we didn't have any luck through our casting agency in New York. We began a search of the A.S.P.C.A., the dog pounds, and dog owners in Connecticut. After three weeks, Bill Berloni, one of the technicians at Goodspeed, located a dog at the Newington Pound that was a day away from being put to sleep. I went to Connecticut that weekend, and after one look said, "Absolutely. That's him." We paid eight dollars and kept him.

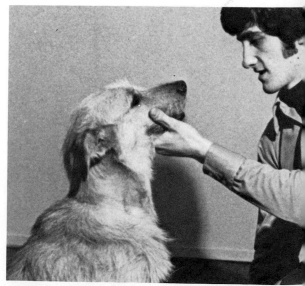

Bill Berloni making
like Lee Strasberg

Andrea McArdle (with hair),
who can hold "Johnny
One-Note"'s note as long
as Ethel Merman can

One of the things we discovered was that Sandy had been mistreated. He was nine months old, and had been severely abused. We didn't know by whom, but we soon learned that whoever it was had worn dark or blue clothing. Sandy was to have two scenes in the musical with policemen, so he had to be carefully and lovingly retrained.

When the company arrived in East Haddam during the week of July 17, I faced an awesome responsibility: to mount a brand new musical in sixteen working days. That was all the rehearsal time we had. It is not the same as doing a revival when you know what the scenes are . . . the stage requirements . . . the songs, when all you have to do is shift some keys around. *Annie* was an original.

Sandy preparing to go on. In order to get him to make one of his cross-overs, an actor drops a piece of bologna in a specific spot on the stage every night. It's probably the most curious stage direction in theatrical history.

Martha Swope

T. Dean Caple, *The Middletown Press*

Martha Swope

The actors had never worked together; I had never worked with any of the people involved; the lines had never been spoken by anyone other than Charles, Tom, and myself; the songs had never been sung by anybody except Charles and me.

I had blocked the entire show in my head. I vaguely knew the traffic, but the second you put people on the stage, the traffic changes, and the space gets cut in a new, three-dimensional way. A great deal of the homework you have done goes out the window.

The Goodspeed stage is the size of a studio apartment in New York City. There is no wing space and the stage is only twenty-three feet from the apron to the back wall. I had worked out a production design concept with Eddie Haynes, the set designer, that utilized every conceivable inch of space. *Dearest Enemy* and *Going Up* had two sets—*Annie* had fourteen set changes!

Sandy having completed a night's work. He takes cabs to the theatre and his house seat location at the Alvin is K-9.
Tom wanted to bill him in the program as "last but not leashed."

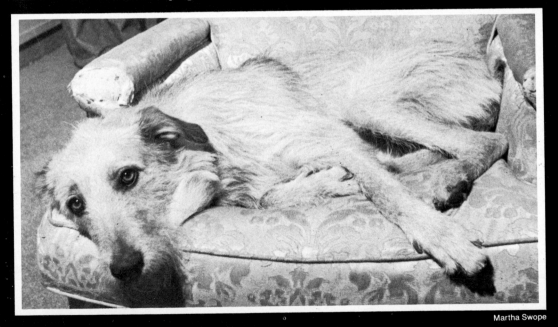

Martha Swope

Charles's original manuscript for "I Don't Need Anything But You,"
with our audition notes on the bottom. It was given to me
in Connecticut as an opening-night present.

Andrea, Danielle, Janine,
and Laura Dean in the
Goodspeed dressing room

We were in rehearsal eight hours a day, and during that frantic period, we all got an education. We had lucked out in that we had hired super-professional actors. The children were remarkable in terms of their memorization capabilities. They knew everything cold within four days. They knew all the songs and every line of the play . . . their own lines and everyone else's lines! The adults worked long and hard with great concentration.

We lived in a strange kind of Brigadoon in East Haddam. Being used to a large city, we had to adjust to life in a small town—three streets, two grocery stores, one restaurant, no movie theatre. The actors lived in boarding houses maintained by the Goodspeed and uninhabited during the winter months. In addition to these accommodations, we also had to locate quarters for the children and their parents or

Andrea, Janine, and Danielle in the pool
at Howard Johnson's motor lodge in Connecticut, just before
they filled it with bubble bath and left for rehearsal

ALL (Cont'd)

(Sing)
YOU'RE ALWAYS
A DAY
AWAY!

"CHANGE
"ALWAYS"
TO
"ONLY"
FOR
REPRISE

(At the end of the number, the
PRESIDENTIAL AIDE enters stage left
with a telegram for ROOSEVELT)

AIDE
Mr. President, an urgent telegram for you.

ROOSEVELT
Ah, yes. Thank you, Harry.
(ROOSEVELT takes the telegram from
the tray and opens it as the AIDE
exits stage left)
Excuse me, everyone.
(ROOSEVELT reads the telegram)
Hmm, Oliver, this isn't for me. It's for you. From your
secretary in New York. "Hundreds of couples jamming street
outside house, all claiming to be Annie's parents. Have
begun to screen them. If possible, please return New York
at once." Signed, Grace Farrell.

FARREL

WARBUCKS
Well, it looks as though "The Hour of Smiles" has more
listeners than we thought, huh, Annie?

ANNIE
Gee. Hundreds of couples. One of them is bound to be my
real mother and father.

ROOSEVELT
Oliver, as much as I'm enjoying your company, and especially
Annie's, I suspect you should get the next train back to New
York.

ANNIE
X TO PRESIDENT

WARBUCKS
(Getting up from the table)
Yes, Franklin, if you don't mind. Annie.

ANNIE
(Getting up from the table)
Yes, Mr. Warbucks. Bye, everybody, it sure was nice to meet
you.
(SHE goes up to ROOSEVELT and kisses
HIM)
And President Roosevelt. Thanks for letting me be here.

CUT

guardians. I lived in a reconditioned apple barn a mile from the theatre and walked to rehearsal each day. But despite the incredibly close living and working conditions, a sense of family, of continuity, started in Connecticut and saw us through the difficult times ahead.

We rehearsed at the theatre, in the public library, on the lawn, at every meal at the restaurant—morning, noon, and night—until August 9, the night of the dress rehearsal when all of the pieces were assembled, and we were as ready as we could possibly be. The actors knew their lines. They knew the intention of the scenes. They knew their blocking. The orchestra had been rehearsed only twice. The sets were claustrophobically trying to creep across the stage. There was just no room. The stagehands were stepping over one another. Most of the detail work still wasn't done, but we were going to have a show.

The theatre is unlike any other entertainment medium. From initial conception to opening night on Broadway, a play undergoes changes. No other medium employs so many talents to bring that "living vehicle" to the stage. You look at the actors. Are they right? You look at the script. Where does it sag? Where is it weak? Where is it not funny enough? You look at the musical numbers. At the energy of the play, not of the actors' performances, but of the play. Is the story being told properly? Is it being serviced by the scenes and the songs? Is there enough entertainment? Is it too heavy in terms of the book? The scenery? The costume changes? Until that Broadway opening, a play is still a work in progress.

A page from an early script.
Grace Farrell was still called Grace Fair
and Miss Hannigan, in this version,
was Miss Asthma.

Phyllis and
Andrea McArdle

Marge and
Shelley Bruce

Marge and
Diana Barrows

Beverly and
Robyn Finn

Kathy and
Janine Rouane

Lorraine and
Donna Graham

Mary and
Danielle Brisebois

That night a major hurricane hit the East Coast, wiping out all of the electricity in New York, Connecticut, and certainly in East Haddam at the Goodspeed Opera House. A local audience had been invited and came despite the storm in progress. We performed that night with a single work light. The air conditioning went off, and the audience walked out forty minutes into the play because they couldn't see and were suffering in the heat. We continued for five and a half hours from the time the lights went out, trying to get through the musical once. The dress rehearsal that started at nine o'clock ended at two in the morning without having finished the second act.

We sent the company home exhausted and scared to death. The stage crew, stage manager, and I stayed up until five o'clock in the morning, and I prayed that the lights would not come on and we would have to cancel the opening night performance. At eleven o'clock that morning the power was restored, and an unfinished *Annie* would have to open.

On opening night the atmosphere backstage was a mixture of anticipation, joy, and fear. The curtain went up at 8:35 and the show lasted three and a half hours. We had never gotten an accurate timing of the show, but I knew we were long. Some of the scene shifts took an inordinate amount of time. One shift lasted eleven minutes. The audience, though impatient, was tolerant. They had been there before and were willing to experience that kind of mistake on an opening night when the cast and crew were still adjusting to a new show.

One thing in our favor was that opening night at Goodspeed is considered a preview night by reviewers. They don't come until four nights into the run. On the

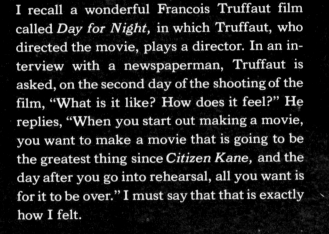

LEAPIN' LIZARDS!

I recall a wonderful Francois Truffaut film called *Day for Night,* in which Truffaut, who directed the movie, plays a director. In an interview with a newspaperman, Truffaut is asked, on the second day of the shooting of the film, "What is it like? How does it feel?" He replies, "When you start out making a movie, you want to make a movie that is going to be the greatest thing since *Citizen Kane,* and the day after you go into rehearsal, all you want is for it to be over." I must say that that is exactly how I felt.

other hand, the audiences see it as opening night. I have never experienced anything like the audiences in Connecticut in my entire life. The people came to East Haddam because they loved the theatre. Approximately 60 percent were on subscription, so, while it was a presold situation, the audiences were both experienced and enthusiastic.

The musical numbers seemed to work . . . the story . . . the characterizations . . . the thrust of the musical. When we came down that night, it was almost everything I had hoped it would be. It was the first time we got any feedback. The audience reaction was quite good considering that our problems were

Bet they col - lect things like ash trays and art. Bet-cha they're good why should - n't they be,
May-be she's made me a clos- et of clothes. May-be they're strict As straight as a line,

Their one mis-take was giv-ing up me. So, may-be now it's time, and
Don't real - ly care as long as they're mine. So, may-be now this prayer's the

may-be when I wake They'll be there call-ing me "Ba - by," May -
last one of it's kind; Won't you please come get your ba - by,

The music department—
Charles with Phil Lang
and Peter Howard

M2605PV02

numerous and staggering. It was two weeks before some of them were solved. Certain cuts were in order, especially for what I call the bladder aspect of a show—no one could be forced to sit in the theatre for three and a half hours with only one intermission. So we had to reduce the amount of playing time from a human standpoint.

The theatre was good acoustically, so sound was not a major problem, and it wasn't necessary to use any amplification. The orchestra consisted of ten pieces, and the only thing we had to make sure of was that the music was not too loud. Phil Lang, who did the orchestrations with Charles, wrote some sparkling arrangements at Goodspeed that ultimately wound up on Broadway. We were correct as far as instrumentation and approach were concerned.

We were now worrying about the weekend when the critics would be coming. Word-of-mouth notwithstanding, we couldn't survive devastating reviews. You want constructive reviews, but you want reviews that are generally on the up side. We got a lot of coverage in Connecticut. It seemed like every tiny town had its own paper and its own theatre critic and we got about thirty-five reviews. Of the thirty-five, twenty were positive, ten were in the middle, and five loathed the show, loathed the idea of it, and made no bones about it. When critics did not like it, they did not like it a lot. Most of the negative reviews were written by reviewers who reacted badly to the concept of the musical. They didn't like the idea of children, dogs, American flags. It was too apple pie . . . too American . . . too obvious . . . too sentimental.

The reviews we really studied were the ones in the middle. I believe you should read reviews the same way you score gymnasts or divers in the Olympics. You get rid of the top and bottom scores and deal with the ones in the middle. That is the way we approached them. We got rid of the wild, enthusiastic, insane raves, and those that said it did not deserve to be up on the stage, and dealt with the ones in the middle.

The Day, New London, Conn., Monday, August 16, 1976

'Annie' is a smash at Goodspeed

By Patricia Mandel
Day Staff Writer

EAST HADDAM — The Goodspeed Opera House has done it again. The world premiere of "Annie," a musical based on Harold Gray's comic strip, "Little Orphan Annie," is a blockbuster of a show.

"Annie" brings to full and vibrant life the winsome orphan and her dog, Sandy; the New York City of the Depression years and President Franklin Delano Roosevelt and the New Deal that are an American tradition in Gray's two-dimensional renderings.

_____ as the hapless 13-year-old Annie gives a performance rare in

GREENWICH TIME.

TUESDAY, AUGUST 17, 1976

Arts

Annie Appeals At Goodspeed

It looks as though Michael Price has fathered another hit. The new show at

rows and Danielle bois. These small all troupers with sional credits.

They are showca song and dance "It's the Hard Knoc which has them about the dingy orp their drab uniform

The orphanage Miss Hannigan, is ing, hardhearted _____ gives just the right amo heavyhandedness placeny, never ove but selfish to the la

Like Goodspee show, "Going "Annie" is chock tuneful songs member, such as "

The New Haven Register

SUNDAY, AUGUST 8, 1976

Leapin' Lizards! I'm 'ANNIE'

Cartoon: Chicago Tribune-New York News Syndicate

Collaborating on the new musical "ANNIE" opening at Goodspeed Opera House on Tuesday are, shown in inset, at the piano, composer Charles Strouse; Thomas Meehan, book; and, leaning on piano, Martin Charnin, lyricist and director. (Photo by Wilson H. Brownell)

BY MARKLAND TAYLOR

EAST HADDAM — "Annie," the new Strouse-Charnin-Meehan musical inspired by Harold Gray's comic strip "Little Orphan Annie," bounces into the Goodspeed Opera House stage here on Tuesday night. Big Deal hopes (and prays) it'll be a big deal.

Big Deal is Martin Charnin, the new musical's lyricist and director. Back in 1957, just two weeks after graduating from Cooper Union, he had one of those lucky breaks that launch some people into the theater. "I read an ad in the New York Times saying that Jerry Robbins was looking for authentic juvenile delinquent types for the original production of 'West Side Story'," he says from behind his shades "I and about 600 others went along to audition. Would you believe I got the part of Big Deal, one of the Jets, sang 'Gee Officer Krupke,' and was paid $275 a week, big money for those days?" Charnin played Big Deal over 1,000 times.

Since then, Charnin has developed into a multiple-threat man. He writes lyrics ("Two by Two," "Hot Spot") and music, directs, makes record albums and singles, writes books, produces and directs nightclub acts, and conceives, produces, directs and writes TV specials. He won a number of Emmys for such specials as "Annie, The Women in the Life of a Man" and "'S Wonderful, 'S Marvelous, 'S Gershwin." In his spare time he came up with the idea for "Annie."

Why did he choose Charles Strouse to write the music? "Because he's the best man for the job, because we're old friends, and because we've been threatening to write a musical together for 15 years." Strouse wrote the scores for "Bye Bye Birdie" and "Applause," winning a Tony for each. He wrote the theme song for TV's "All ..."

... for such films ... "The Night ... Those are just l ... Next, Ch ... write the book ... han filled the ... writer on The N ... and still contri ... pieces to it. He ... Playboy and th ... Magazine, too. ... cal sketches for ...

Annie comes alive

LEE PARKHURST

... we've been reading about ... me has come alive on ... Goodspeed Opera House ... ng the hearts of all those

... phan Annie" was born in ... by Harold Gray who laid ... ndation for the enduring ... ow the "little orphan" ... a brand new home built by ... rouse (music), Martin ... lics), and Thomas Meehan ... musical

continuing the story line to a great extent. The songs are generally catchy, tuneful and lilting, with some staying and lingering with you after the show. This is not surprising considering Martin Charnin has previously collaborated with Richard Rodgers on "Two By Two" and Charles Strouse gave us some memorable music with "Applause" and "Bye, Bye Birdie." Especially likable to this reviewer was "It's The Hard Knock Life," the ... "We Got Annie," the stirring "Tomorrow" (reminiscent of ...

with Meehan's book and ... which does not seem to be ... as Act One. From the chang ... in the order of the music ... with additions and omission ... is undoubtedly still goo ... "tryouts." As the run co ... sure things will become b

Also, at this point, the s ... not change smoothly enoug ... many locales are involved ... making many sets ... Therefore, the staging of th ... could be one of the probl

THE MIDDLETOWN (CONN.) PRESS

'Annie' Opens

"Annie," book by Thomas Meehan. ic by Charles Strouse, lyrics by in Charnin. Featuring Andrea urdie, Reid Shelton, and Sandy on. Directed by Martin Charnin, reography by Dan Siretta, musical ction by Lynn Crigler. Produced ichael P. Price. At the Goodspeed ra House.

By D'VERA COHN

hey had a purpose in not ing critics in the aisle s." a fellow reviewer re- ked from mid-row during mission at the Goodspeed

seats and endure the first half of the performance, they will find the second half all delightful.

"Annie" starts off loo ... like an empty, somew ... shabby apartment about w ... one remarks that it has po ... tial It ends leaving the a ... dience regretting that it ... so long to realize it

The musical tells the s

A

of prod ... a nice ... be patro ... It is

'Annie' Gives Unco

By RICHARD CONWAY

ncomfortable. That is the feeling I had from the f the Goodspeed Opera House's new to the final curtain call. The feeling ly home and still leaves an unsatisfying

... roduction, ... tried to ... character ... average ... es in the

times, one thinks that the interpretation of the early long-running comic strip.

At other times, g ven t the characters are as ed t characterizations dire tor C feels that perhaps a c mp in

During the final coup President Roosevelt - he sh home of Daddy Warb cks f that their real parents are de offer but the platitude abo happy ending. One winced the seat.

The Hartford Courant

AUGUST 22, 1976

Stage/Goodspeed's Sad 'Annie'

By MALCOLM L. JOHNSON

It is showtime but the audience is still milling about outside the elegant white swan of a theater on Goodspeed's Landing, glancing over from time to time at the men at work near the yellow Connecticut Light and Power Co. truck near the bridge.

an eclectic grabbag of tunes, and from the start it is clear that this "Annie" is really "Oliver!" in drag, lost in Depression America.

But although Lionel Bart's adaptation of Dickens had neither the strength of the original nor the integrity of a more fully realized musical show, it truly towers over this American stepchild — in the writing s, in its songs, in its settings.

most nothing works. If has had the stuff her; as conceived in mas Meehan and the n Charnin, she is a y little tot, but with- 's feisty confidence, on sense, straightfor ently workable phi and shrewd human

Charnin Annie is a one who could have fraction of the hair that Gray sent the more than 40 years. her, but not so fortu audience, she really ich to go up against eventless book that ovided. Or to put it ere isn't a Fagan or ht

Annie contains only iguing conceit: that m — as outlined in a nd lively tune called helped get Franklin d his cabinet out of d into the positive

The show does have a couple of tolerable moments: the FDR gang warming to "Tomorrow" and the upbeat "You're Never Fully Dressed Without a Smile" on a mildly diverting parody of early radio. It isn't

... at the au ... w to be. At

20—The Morning Record, Meriden, Conn., Monday, Au

HAVE YOU SEEN...

'Annie' at Goodsp

The new musical "Annie" now playing at the Goodspeed Opera House in East Haddam is a comic invention scripted by Thomas Meehan on the basis of the familiar comic strip Orphan Annie.

tunes and some attractive people, among them Annie herself and Daddy Warbucks, along with characters representing Franklin Delano Roosevelt, J. Edgar Hoover, Bernard Baruch, Harold

THE CHRISTIAN SCIENCE MONITOR
August 24, 1976

day. E drels to ing as thwart cept th ever al adopte makes on stag Andr the pa lightful happy child s show. pealing comic Meehan made i

Little Orphan Annie — now a musical heroine

Goodspeed Opera's 'Annie' shows her before curls and cartoon fame

By Thor Eckert Jr.

East Haddam, Co Little Orphan Annie as the heroine of a sical?

"Annie," the Goodspeed Opera House's f production — and its new musical for the y — is just that. Two of Goodspeed's new m cals have seen Broadway lights - "So thing's Afoot," and "Shenandoah" Others h deservedly faded away.

Theater

"Annie" needs work, but it already has much that works Charles Strouse plause") has concocted a wonderful sco Martin Charnin, who also directs, some stu amusing lyrics. "Annie" is the story of

for now, almost sinks the show. When Grace

Straw Hat Theatre

The Advocate, Wednesday, August 18, 1976.

HEATER ..

Annie brings nostalgic fun to Goodspeed audiences

By LYNN DEAN

a cartoon comic format as a a musical has provided a few uctions in the past. "You're a lan, Charlie Brown" is a good point, so is the musical centered dventures of "Superman." Both attendance records while light-hearted fun for total consumptio die on the l ng piece, strip "Lit being oner fouse in Eas s to be an ur e stops are an equal n Daddy W s pack as e crabby, nnigan, get as overseei also a chon n wrap on as they sir

plays Oliver Warbucks with all the dash, verve and sentimental characterization intact. Mr. Shelton bounces around the stage in an electrifying manner that activates all the players around him. He delivers some of the best lines in the play along with that classic about everything west of New York City being like Bridgeport.

Annie, Sandy, Daddy Warb Win Your Heart At G

Annie, a musically interpreted production of Thomas Meehan's book, is currently being presented at the Goodspeed Opera House in East Haddam. Martin Charnin directs this production for which he also

class which poses such questions as "What's the soup D'jour today?", but she doesn't exactly please the Bixbys. Annie makes plans to run away with Sandy, a shaggy stray dog, but ends up back in the orphanage. In December of 1933 Annie is

Barbar three rob her cha gravel-pl Last, but the orpha the happ as the lit

Herald Review:

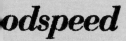

One thing that wasn't working in
Connecticut was the way Annie was being
played. The language didn't change from
Goodspeed to Washington, the actress
changed. The first little girl we had hired
was vulnerable, pretty, sensitive, but didn't
have the one quality that Annie really
needed—that street-smart spunk that
attracted us to the character to begin with.

We had gone soft in our casting. I
realized it ten days after we were in
rehearsal, and broached the subject to Tom
first, and then to Charles. Tom couldn't
contemplate such a drastic move. Charles
reacted similarly, but knew that something
had to be done. Among the three of us, we
decided to wait. There was so much chaos it
would have been a mistake to have done
anything at that point.

On Sunday night, after the first week of
performances, I decided I had to let the
youngster go. I checked it out with Price,
who spoke to her first, and then talked with
her mother. I had never fired anyone in my
entire life, and the notion of letting her go
was frightening to me. How do you fire a
thirteen-year-old child? But, it had to be
done. Her vulnerability, an asset in the
beginning, was seriously hurting the playing
of all the street-wise scenes—the ones that
were already in the play, and the ones we
were writing into it. I was demolished by the
whole thing, but I had no choice.

A Spunky Orphan Hits the Stage—

Will 'Annie' Make It to Broadway?

By TIM HOLLEY
Post Theater Editor

EAST HADDAM — "'Annie' is the kind of musical that feeds on everyone's desire for Jimmy Carter to win," director Martin Charnin boasted after a matinee last week.

Blowing a thousand and one trumpets about his new

integrity of the Grey characters. But we invented the plot in regard to Annie's meeting Warbucks and Sandy, and the how and why of their love story, realizing that her search for her real parents and his conflict about finding them was the meat of the musical.

dealt with in the strip. We've invented the tale of the kid looking for a real family and finding a surrogate father. The scene with Annie inspiring the New Deal is not in the original cartoon. The New Deal and Roosevelt and his cabinet came in contact with the cartoon only by implication, not by

e Are Problems, But Show Holds Promise

Annie' At The Goodsp Diamond In The Ro

now a dissenting opinion "Annie," the new musi- w in its world premiere ment at the Goodspeed House in East H senting from bo had rave review ablished a few da New Haven R e super - critics that appeared in d Courant and pecially the latte

write it off as potential Broadway fare, even a possible hit. I have seen worse there, much

scenes complete some of the are at least

as orphans, a new an nding. The story ta rom mistreatment i rk City orphanage eceived by Presid Roosevelt and m ne, bears title re so either the comic a awned it or to really at face value, the p mas Meehan is go surd even for the 19 e musical score

The New Haven Register
SUNDAY, AUGUST 29, 1976

2 'Arfs' For 'Annie' (Work In Progress)

By MARKLAND TAYLOR

EAST HADDAM — "Annie," the current production at the Goodspeed Opera House, is a brand new musical. As such, like it or not, it's a work in progress, a production suffering birth pangs. At the end of the first week of its seven-week run "Annie" was still a clumsy baby, unfocused and wobbly. On Tuesday night, after a cast change in its title role and a second week of performances and constant work, it was much more assured. The first week of any new musical are, inevitably, weeks of cutting, changing and rewriting.

"Tomorrow" borrows some of the insistent beat of rock. Elsewhere there are aptly mournful wails and schmalzy violin solos. Great fun, conducted by Lynn Crigler with sureness and elan, as always.

At the end of the first week, however, Strouse's score was surrounded by clutter. Virtually every scene went on long after its point was made, and both book and scenery needed ruthless trimming; they were constantly bringing "Annie" to a halt. Of all musicals, "Annie" shouldn't talk itself to death or be laden with heavy acts (the denouement is still far too talkative). It should have the succinct

artford Weekender Times
Friday, August 20, 1976   17

he Goodspeed has an 'orphan'

LEN J. HONEYMAN
ADDAM — Not even Daddy can have Little Orphan Annie

ven a strong second-act open- ve "Annie," the Goodspeed e's third offering this season. es Strouse — Martin Charnin book by Thomas Meehan,

doesn't go anywhere. It isn't Little Orphan Annie of the comics, it isn't social commentary, it just wanders across two acts.
With the exception of "Tomorrow," a

which plays himself, is staged at board level. Down on the stage, where no one except first-row sitters can see. That's a no-no which I was surprised to see at a house

funnies

ng

ppened

THEATER/
ATRICIA O'HAIRE

RE IS a delightful tory line hidden somewhere in "An- new musical being these nights at al Goodspeed Opera in East Haddam, Conn. rtunately, writer Meehan and his col.

At Goodspeed

OH!

OH, SANDY- IT IS TRUE- ALL THESE CLIPPINGS PROVE IT---

8-17-36

eechman, Harriett Conrad, onald Craig, Richard En- llen, Barbara Erwin, aymond Thorne, Diana arrows, Danielle Brisebois, mie Ruane, ddie Cowan, , Mallory incus, David Sandy

Riddled with excelle and bits of hum melodrama, the pr moves smoothly and pace to a happy conclu Martin Charnin's direct Crigler's musical direc be applauded but at volume renders the

---

Andrea McArdle was a serious contender for the part of Annie from the first day of rehearsal. I talked to Phyllis McArdle, her mother, before the Sunday performance and asked whether she thought Andrea could play the leading role. She did.

At the end of the performance I took Andrea aside and sat her down on my knee. She seemed very, very small. I had my arms around her, holding her in a way that I have held my own daughter so many times. I said to her, "Andrea, I want you to take over the part. I want you to be Little Orphan Annie." She started to cry, and then asked about the young actress she would be replacing.

I told Andrea I wanted her to be ready for the role on Tuesday night. The brave little kid said okay. She went to have dinner, and at 8:30 Sunday night we started to work on the score. The songs were in the right key, so we didn't have to do any reorchestration . . . and she knew them cold. She wasn't sure about the blocking. We worked all day Monday, the cast's day off, talking—talking about the part, talking about the lines, rehearsing the lines. We worked again on Tuesday, and then did a run-through that afternoon with the company.

Andrea played Annie for the first time that night and the show changed for everyone. The focus of the musical was suddenly in place. Charles and Tom and I were absolutely delighted. We sensed a totally different reaction from the audience. What had been an interested reaction became a good reaction, a better than good reaction. At that moment it was apparent that a major problem had been solved and that Andrea would be our Annie.

There was an indication the second week that the show's word of mouth was quite good. That meant the audience was going away feeling happy, talking positively about the show. The phones were ringing at the Goodspeed box office, and Price decided to extend the show three weeks beyond the ten-week run.

We worked relentlessly for the next eleven weeks, fixing, changing, shifting, moving a song from one scene to the next, rewriting, throwing out a musical number, trying to solve a script problem, trying to solve a piece of characterization. Most of our attention was addressed to Oliver Warbucks, because we hadn't been able to unshackle ourselves from Harold Gray. We were still wearing two hats: the hat of our Warbucks and that of Gray's Warbucks. That undefined Warbucks is the character Walter Kerr, the influential *New York Times* critic, saw when he came to see *Annie* on August 27.

The name "Ann" has always been lucky for me. The first television special I conceived and produced starred the incomparable Bancroft, and was called "Annie: The Women in the Life of a Man." Two specials later, I decided to cast nothing but Anns in my television version of "Dames at Sea," Anns whose last names began with the letter "m". "Dames" aired with Anne Meara, Ann Miller, and Ann-Margaret in the leading roles. *Annie*, of course, is played by Andrea McArdle.

STAGE VIEW
WALTER KERR

Nothing's Comic About 'Anni

id you ever have the feeling of bein
dislocated in the theater, so that on
you seemed to know exactly where you
time and space and the very next yo
yourself on the down escalator going up?
that feeling rather often last week at the charm
ing Goodspeed Opera House in East Haddam, Conn., where a
agreeable but ideologically treacherous new musical
of "Little Orphan Annie' being given its formal
iting, or perhaps rely tolerant, world.
ave up the "funnies" lo s ago, you
r the Harold Gray comic-strip the
d "Annie" has now been derived. A
og S ndy and her benefactor Daddy Warbucks, a
blind a bats if you were to judge by the empty
served of them as eyes. All of them, Sandy p
excepted, extremely pontifical, not at all interested in be
funny if a le moralizing, or a *lot* of moralizing, could b
squo to the busy balloons And the sociology itself
ly oriented: somewhere to the far right of Genghis
in, so much so that Franklin Delano Roosevelt de-
ed on running fo another four years (I forget wheth
it was the thir ourth term) the saintly Daddy Warb
killed himself ther than endure the prospect. (He rise
from the d ter, but we can't go into all th
e you could say that in most w poser
Strouse, lyricist Martin Charnin brettist
Thomas Meehan have been faithful to the ong-beloved
source. They are stymied on one point, o ourse. Actors
have eyes, and eyes reflect personalities, and personalities
tend to be likable unless they are absolutely *forced* to make
themselves loathsome for plot purposes—which means that

you've got a figure o can admire, even cher
Pretty much the sam r Reid Shelton, who
the mysterious Oli Varbucks. Mr. Shelt
such a gentle smil a mannerly way wi
waltzes a f he living room
you quite f money or how
wish him a s

ng prob n that comes
original without exactly being
the socio-political sphe (fancy
at are you going to do w "ittle
specifically i

I n a summer stock situation, a good review from someone like Walter Kerr can
propel you into a Broadway production. A bad review can theoretically kill you, stop
you cold. We didn't want Kerr to come at that point. We knew we were not ready.
Price insisted. Kerr came. We gave him a good performance. He gave us a bad
review.

His main point had to do with the politics of Oliver Warbucks. In effect, he said
we had better get our house in order. He pointed out something that was confusing to
him, and, I guess, confusing to the audiences. We were demolished by the review,
and hoped it wouldn't affect the potential move to New York. It happened early
enough in the run for us to take some of his thoughts into account in our revisions.

Culver Pictures

Did W[arb]ucks invent the New Deal?

SUNDAY, SEPTEM[BER ... 5,] 1976   D   5

But we don't and we aren't. Not a bit. First thing [you] know Daddy Warbucks is walking down the charco[al-]littered streets of the Depression — a background [that] mysteriously, to represent Fifth Avenue during a [...] praise to glorious New York City — and becomin[g ...] [...] sees. Next thing you kno[w ...] on [...] to vario[us ...] the Presi[dent ...] "new idea," a deve[lopment ...] we follow it — make[s ...] sponsible for the entire N[...]

Nor is that quite all. Soo[n ...] [b]ursting i[n ...] ings with his 13-year-old c[...] ("[...]") mind if Annie sits in on th[e ...] brighten up a thoroughly disr[...] [...]dell the-dumps Harold Ickes, [...] [thor]oughly H[o]over [...] hopping on[...] reassuring [...] song [...] e out [...] rrow." F. D. R. [...] himself in [...] Christmas party, [ciga]rette-holder [...], bosom friend [...] [new]ly formed family. (F.D.R., by the way, is perfectly [...]ed, not overplayed, by Raymond Thorne.) The whol[e thing] [en]ds up with everybody singing "A New Deal for Christmas."

Well, now. Nobody really expects a musical to e[...] [...] or even to incl[u]de, the spectacle of the nicest fello[w] [...] premises doing a[way] with himself (as Daddy Warbucks [...]) "I believe that all s[tori]es, especially these days, should ha[ve] happy endings"). No[t ...] that. [...] one does, somehow or other, expect even a musi[cal ...] its guns (or should I say munitions?). You can do [...] g more or less true to a period feel and philosophy, [...] [...] feel and phil-osophy may have been. You can do it H[arold] Gray's way if you'll do it that way. Or you can do parod[y], purposefully kidding a onetime state of mind. You can pro[bably d]o other things. What you can't do is slip and slide [...] one point of view to another, rather as though the o[...] [...] with [t]heir pails and scrub-brushes had soaped the f[...] [...] for [...] to rinse and dry it, leaving it quite a peril [...] [...] and social security.

[...]s all right (he's bigger than Annie). And there's [...] the littlest, the best tap-dancer and the only [...] i[n th]e bunch — whose name is Danielle Brisboise, a[nd w]hom I [w]ould like to mention because if she's ever up for adoption, [I'm] here.

Daddy, in [...], ta[...] from [...] [la]vish g[...] [g]iving to make it beamingly cle[ar] that he is ruthless, having [fo]ught his way up from Hell's Kitchen himself. "You don't have to be nice to people on the way up," he announces, "if you're not

---

The previous season, Walter Kerr's review of *Shenandoah* was largely responsible for bringing the show to Broadway. Kerr gave it a glowing review, which I'm certain was instrumental in raising the additional money to bring the musical to New York.

At the same time Walter Kerr was saying we had better get our politics straight, Andrea was making the role her own, and all of the surrounding material was being structured and strengthened. Suddenly, the audiences began to stand up at the end of the performances and cheer. Not only were they cheering, but they were laughing hilariously and crying at the right places. Someone once said that if you can make them laugh, you can run a year. If you can make them cry, you can run two years. If you can make them laugh and cry, you can run forever.

There is another crucial moment in this adventure. What would happen to *Annie* when we closed at the Goodspeed in October? In April, before going to Connecticut, I had met Irwin Meyer and Stephen R. Friedman, who were quite enamored of the property and wanted to do their first Broadway show. They had signed Dramatist Guild contracts with Charles, Tom, and myself just at the time we opened in August. But now in September, their belief in the play was seriously threatened by the negative reviews. Walter Kerr's review had said, in effect, that the show didn't work and there wasn't a chance we would make it in New York.

There was a two-week period directly after Kerr's review when our future looked bleak. The play was getting better . . . the audiences were cheering and yelling and carrying on. But, as the show was improving, the likelihood of our going to Broadway was diminishing. At that time Lewis Allen entered the picture. A friend of Charles Strouse, Lewis had worked with Charles on a show called *I and Albert* in London. Lewis and his wife Jay Presson Allen came up to see *Annie* in September, and told Charles that night that it was absolutely spectacular. That lifted his spirits, and mine too when he reported their conversation to me. Lewis then requested that his partner Mike Nichols come to see the show.

Mike and his then very pregnant wife Annabel came up to me before the performance and, as Mike has often said, had the same apprehension and attitude that Tom had had: "Who wants to see anything about Little Orphan Annie?"

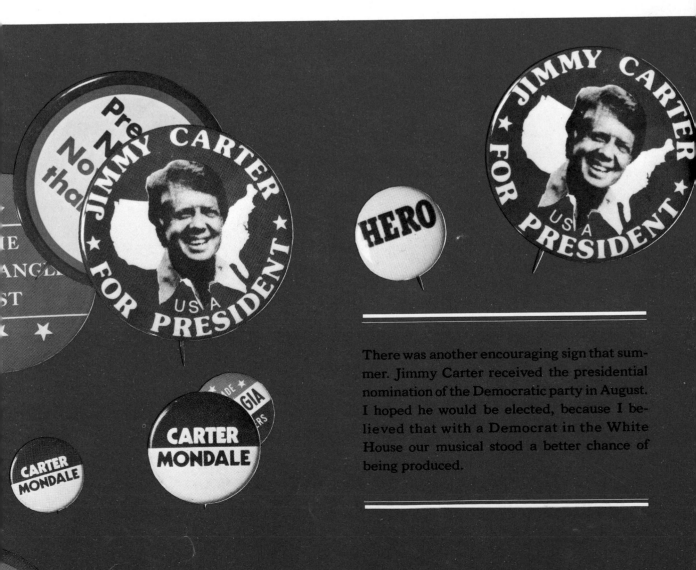

There was another encouraging sign that summer. Jimmy Carter received the presidential nomination of the Democratic party in August. I hoped he would be elected, because I believed that with a Democrat in the White House our musical stood a better chance of being produced.

The Gelston House Restaurant—the only game in town.
There's a back room where we all gathered after performances
and sang until one or two in the morning. Every time
I left, the children were still going strong.

Mike Nichols

I asked them to have a drink with me afterward to get his professional reaction
to the property. Later at the Gelston House, Mike and Annabel were in tears. They
told me *Annie* was absolutely the best musical that has ever been. "Don't be
discouraged by any of the things that are discouraging you," Mike said. "If I were a
producer, I would do it in a second."

They returned to New York and the next morning I got a telephone call from
Irwin Meyer saying that Lewis Allen and Mike Nichols had decided they wanted to
produce *Annie* as a Broadway musical with Meyer and Friedman. It was literally
overnight that Nichols became one of the producers of the musical, and the moment
he became involved, everyone's attitude changed. "Oh my goodness, maybe there
really is something in that thing if Mike Nichols has decided to do it!"

Nichols was wildly supportive in the course of the remaining weeks at
Goodspeed. When we got back to New York, he functioned in the best way a
producer can function, by giving us a free hand in reworking the musical and
forming an invisible wall against the other problems attendant to putting on the
show. He said, "Put the musical on the way you guys want it and I'll field all the
other problems." He said he wanted to be the kind of producer he never had as a
director. He was supportive; he was very helpful to Tom and Charles and me. We
would spitball ideas with him, we would pick his brains when he was available to us,
and he went about the business of raising the money with Lewis while we continued
our work on the show.

INTERMISSION:
Something Was Missing

We went back into New York after Goodspeed and began to raise the necessary new money for the Broadway production. Our values changed between the time we closed in Connecticut and opened in Washington due to the fact that we were now mounting a major musical, a musical of great size . . . a million-dollar musical. *Annie* cost about $70,000 to put on in Connecticut. On Broadway, *Annie* ultimately cost $1,000,000.

A new budget had to be drawn up. Once we examined the script and determined the size of the production—in our case, 20 musicians, 16 sets, 185 costumes—we then had to deal with the requirements of the unions. Fees and salaries had to be added for stagehands, electricians, sound personnel, press agents, general managers, company managers, advertising personnel.

The money had to be raised. To capitalize a show, a limited partnership is formed. The limited partners invest for a share of the profits. For *Annie,* the initial Broadway budget was $650,000; units were sold for as little as $1,500. We were able to get the show capitalized with about thirty people putting up the entire amount.

FUNNY HOW TH'
THINGS YUH WANT
MOST ARE TH'
HARDEST TO ASK FOR–

The Hooverville scene in an early stage at the Broadway Arts rehearsal studio, and then on the stage of the Eisenhower

rtha Swope
rtha Swope

We redesigned and recostumed the musical and reorchestrated a great deal of it. The show was now going into a house with twenty musicians, as compared with ten at Goodspeed. We needed a larger company. We still had some book things to work on.

We had one scene that took place in a Beanery and we tried to rewrite it six or eight times. During the hiatus period between the time we came back from Connecticut and the time we went into rehearsal in January, it was rewritten three additional times. Finally, the week before we went into rehearsal, the Beanery scene became Hooverville. A new musical number was added later. The song that was originally in that spot, in fact the first written for the show, was "We Got Annie." After perhaps twenty lyric

rewrites we finally, reluctantly, threw it out. Charles and I, in an afternoon, wrote "We'd Like to Thank You Herbert Hoover." It went into rehearsal the following day and ultimately stopped the show in Washington. As we worked on the music, Tom was restructuring the book. Before we had locked into any musical numbers, we had to slug them into the scenes. Tom would often have to write the musical number in in a different way than he had originally intended.

From the time the first draft of the musical was written until the time we opened on Broadway, I would say that no more than 25 percent of the musical was changed. These changes occurred for any number of reasons. When you write a scene for a musical, somewhere in the middle of the scene, you are going for a song—a character song, a piece of sheer entertainment, or something that furthers the story. Sometimes the musical numbers don't work, and changes are needed when the composer and lyricist have not been able to lock into a song successfully. Sometimes, you can redo a musical number, but Charles and I found that the easiest way to approach a song that didn't work was to throw it out entirely and start over. We would look for an entirely new concept . . . a new tempo . . . a new rhyme scheme.

Charles Strouse and I had a collaboration that was very much the way I like to work. We would sit in the same room and try things out on each other. I would read a line of lyric and he would set it instantly at the piano. Once the lyric had a tune, it also had a rhythmic structure. I would then develop the lyric and he would adjust the melody. It was like playing catch with an unformed song. When we agreed the idea was good enough, we would go our separate ways to complete the lyric and the melody, and then get together to work on the fine points of the song. It was a very loose, yet complete, collaboration. Ours was not a typical working relationship. Working together can be difficult. You are exposing yourself, in a sense. The work process is often a private thing. People like to work alone, to lie on the couch and look up at the ceiling, chew on pencils and use a lot of yellow pads, and take hours to write lyrics or privately hammer away at the piano to get a tune going.

When I was writing *Two by Two* with Richard Rodgers we worked separately. Once the librettist Peter Stone and I had decided what the responsibility of the musical number was to be, I would then structure the lyric. It was turned over to Rodgers, who would bring me a finished song a few days later. Most of the collaborations I know about are this way: The composer and lyricist investigate the scene together, decide what they want to do, and go their separate ways.

I think the reason the *Annie* score holds up so well is because we worked together.

The three musketeers on the promenade of the Eisenhower Theatre.
The Watergate is in the background.

The score for a musical has to be programmed. You can't have five consecutive ballads or five consecutive solo numbers. You have to deal deliberately with each number, and layer it. You start with the opening song and layer the next musical number on it, and layer the third number on it, and layer and layer and layer until you end up with an act. Then, everyone takes a deep breath, and begins work on the second act.

In every musical there are book songs—songs that do nothing other than further the action of the play. Inside the magic of a musical number you can accomplish more than you can in a book scene, for the audience's enjoyment is doubled when they get information through song. Sometimes the worst kinds of songs on the stage are the "hits"—songs that literally stop the action cold, because it is apparent that the composer and the lyricist have decided this is going to be a hit song. This is the song that everybody is ultimately going to record. It has nothing to do with furthering the plot or exposing the character. It may have a wonderful melody or an ingenious lyric, but it may leave the audiences cold. They become disinterested, and stop paying attention. Oscar Hammerstein, for example, had a great gift. Oscar was able to create a lyric that would work exactly inside the fabric of the scene but could be taken out of the context of the musical and sung as a song.

Laurie Beechman, Reid, Dick Ensslen, Andrea, Jim Hosbein,
Ray Thorne, and Bob Freschi rehearsing the Cabinet scene in New York,
and then in costume, with make-up, on stage at the Eisenhower.

Singing along with Sandy

We made a creative decision early on that we wanted to give the audience a musical loaded with production values. It would be a feast for the eyes. The audiences were going to get their money's worth. I was tired of seeing actors sitting on stools, asking the audience to do so much filling in. I wanted the setting to be realistic. I didn't want it to be a basic unit set.

The decision to hire David Mitchell and Theoni Aldredge as set designer and costume designer took place in November. Theoni had done many of the shows for Joseph Papp at the New York Shakespeare Festival, designed the costumes for *Hair* and *Chorus Line*, and had designed costumes for films, winning an Academy Award for *The Great Gatsby*. I had worked with Theoni on eight projects before *Annie*—five of them on television and three on Broadway. I hadn't worked with Mitchell, but he had worked for Joe Papp and knew Theoni quite well.

Mitchell and I talked at great length about the new set for *Annie*. It is complicated with unique treadmill moves and many set-pieces that fly. We had to build a deck and construct two treadmills. We also decided that each setting in the musical was going to materialize on the stage. We weren't going to do any cheats. A velour drape wasn't going to come in, and we wouldn't do any cross-overs in one. The audience would be given a designed show from top to bottom.

For the New York skyline scenes, Mitchell went to the New York Public Library, to the Bettman Archives, and other sources to get pictorial references from the thirties. Every building that became a photo blow-up in the show comes authentically from someplace in New York in the thirties. Whereas Boris Aronson's designs for *Fiddler on the Roof* were influenced by Chagall, Edward Hopper was our source— Hopper's New York.

David Mitchell's miniature models for the set,
taken from authentic 1930s New York photographs.
We played with these cutouts for hours on end
to get the right positions for the stage.

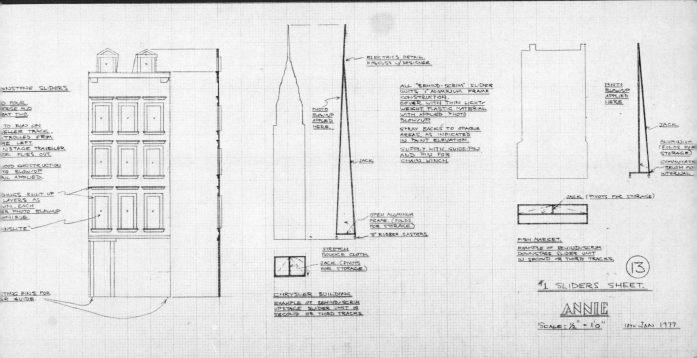

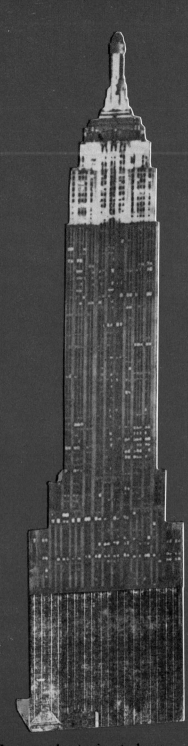

We were also trying to keep something of Harold Gray's shading in the sets. Gray was a master of light and dark. His colors and shapes were very apparent, very obvious, very flat. Black was black, white was white, and we thought we could accomplish this with lighting. Our lighting designer, Judy Rasmuson, developed a light plot that gave us these darks and lights.

As complicated as the moves are, with practice the set moves faultlessly. During the early practice, however, Warbucks's statue of Venus de Milo once ended up in the middle of Times Square and one night the orphange was the home of Mona Lisa.

The orphanage set being put into place by the crew. The doors ride in on treadmills and stop at specific marks to meet the walls, which fly in from above...inches count.

Jack Timmers at the stage manager's desk, running the show. The television camera is on during the performance shooting the entire action of the play so the stage managers have a total view of the action onstage.

T hen Mitchell and I took our thoughts to Mike Nichols. He agreed wholeheartedly with what we were doing, and we realized it could never be done for the kind of dollars we had allotted. The set for the Broadway production ended up costing $185,000—a lot of money for a set.

The costumes were another expensive item in the budget. Theoni and I decided that the costumes weren't going to be secondhand; we wouldn't do a lot of thrift-shop buying. She was going to design the clothes, and they would be executed by Barbara Matera's costume shop. Again, we were going to give the audience their money's worth.

Theoni's original costume
sketches, drawn with
great attention to detail.
She has a peculiar
habit of delivering
everything promised.

In November, we began a series of weekly backers' auditions in order to get more people into the project. At this point, Sam Cohn, an agent for International Creative Management, became involved through his clients Mike Nichols and Lewis Allen. Sam worked long and hard on the property. He was instrumental in making certain deals work for us, in contract negotiations, in theatre negotiations. Sam believed in the show and wanted to see it done properly. He became one of our most avid supporters.

Hirschfeld's cartoon of Sam Cohn as Little Orphan Annie. Commissioned by Mike Nichols, he presented it to Sam on opening night in New York.

At that time she had her own night club act. She had played throughout the country, and was very successful in New York. As a matter of fact, the first time I saw her she was starring at the Blue Angel, and the opening act consisted of two newcomers named Mike Nichols and Elaine May, fresh from Chicago, who did improvisations. Mike knew Dorothy quite well and concurred that she would be ideal for the Hannigan role.

La Loudon in action

Some recasting also had to be done. One of the places where we were not servicing the material as well as we could was in the character of Miss Hannigan. The actress at Goodspeed didn't have the comedic equipment we believed was necessary to make Miss Hannigan into an extravagant, eccentric character in the play, and so I suggested that Dorothy Loudon audition for the role.

Three or four years before, when we first talked about Miss Hannigan, the possibility of having Dorothy play the part was discussed.

Dorothy did a cold reading of some of the newly written Hannigan scenes. Her audition was incredibly funny, bawdy, riotous. We offered her the role.

Martha S

There was a little contract negotiation. Her late husband, Norman Paris, who was a fine musician, was instrumental in convincing Dorothy she coud play Miss Hannigan, that she could be mean, and that the audiences would love to hate her. This is exactly what happened. Dorothy is brilliant in the role; it is a triumph of characterization.

Rehearsals were to start at Christmas. In December, Andrea called me from Philadelphia with the news that she had mononucleosis. Merry Christmas! But we were still raising money, and fortunately for us the rehearsals had to be postponed until the middle of January, and Andrea was able to go on.

It was at this time that Reid shaved his head. I wanted him to do it early, so we could see how the character of Warbucks would play with a bald head, as Gray had originally invented him. Reid arrived at the first rehearsal bald. He had shaved his head for his role in *The Rothschilds,* but told me he had felt uncomfortable without hair. Caring for a bald head can be a nuisance. If you are not naturally bald, you have to get a good razor to get rid of the fuzz. He agreed to shave his head only if the company bought him a three-headed Norelco. And this we did.

Vincent Minnelli was the director of a spectacular disaster I was associated with in 1967 called *Mata Hari.* It was a serious antiwar musical written with considerable skill by Jerome Coopersmith (libretto) and Edward Thomas (music) and produced by David Merrick. I wrote the lyrics. Pernell Roberts, released from years of starring on "Bonanza," played the male lead, and Mata Hari was portrayed by an exquisite German girl named Marissa Mell. The musical was plagued with trouble from the first day when Minnelli, who was returning to Broadway after twenty years in Hollywood, gathered his actors together to rehearse at the Cort Theatre, put the people on the stage for the first scene, took a seat in the fifth row of the darkened house, and called out "Action!" For some unexplained reason, Merrick opened the musical in Washington, and to make matters worse, the first preview was a benefit for either the Marine Corps or the American Legion. It wasn't fashionable in 1967 to protest Vietnam directly or indirectly, and the reception that evening was comparable to a performance of *Fiddler on the Roof* in Cairo. We never got to New York. Merrick turned off the lights on us in Washington. But, each day during our run at the National Theatre, I would hang out in the wings or the basement waiting for some miracle to prevent the closing. One rainy afternoon I ran into Irene Sharaff, who had designed the costumes for the show, and she said to me, "You're really a theatre rat!"

It's true. I'd rather be in the theatre working than any place in the world. I'd rather be out of town in trouble with a musical than producing a night club act, directing a television show, or winning an award.

Bill Yoscary

© Jill Krementz

Arf waiting in the wings.
Why am I reminded of Eve Harrington?

Janet Beroza, *Annie*'s production stage manager,
eavesdropping on a private moment between two stars

When we got back to New York from Connecticut, Bill Berloni took Sandy to
Captain Haggarty's dog-training school on Seventy-sixth Street in Manhattan, where
Sandy was taught the six tricks he had to perform. The first one, quite simply, is that
he has to be pushed out on stage on cue. He goes to the mark where he meets Annie,
and when she says to him, "Did they hurt you?" he has to roll over. In his next scene he
lies on his back and ignores the actors when they talk about him and use his name. Then
he does respond when Annie calls him. He jumps up and puts his paws on her shoulders.

 The last trick he has to do, the most difficult, is to walk across an empty
stage. In one scene Annie and Sandy run away, and she is caught and brought back
to the orphanage. Sandy escapes and looks for Annie all over the city. He has to walk
from stage left to stage right—it is a cross-over on a bare stage, and he has to do it in
time to the music. He is incredible. He has never been naughty on the stage.
Sometimes he misses his cue because his attention span is short, but the one crucial
trick, that important one of walking across, sitting down and slowly doing a Jack
Benny take to the audience—he does that perfectly every time.

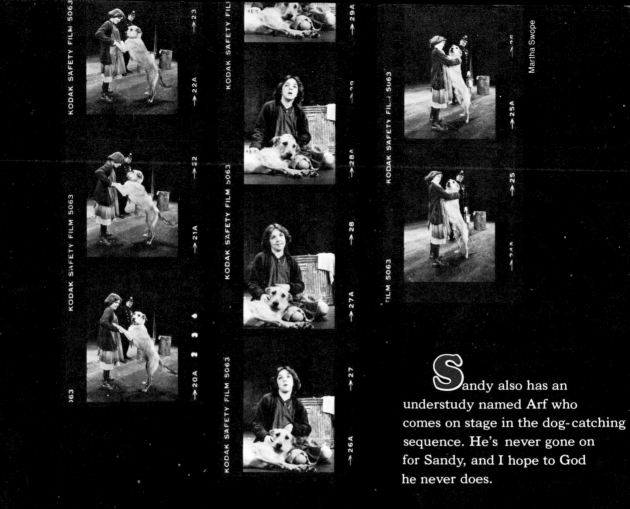

Sandy also has an understudy named Arf who comes on stage in the dog-catching sequence. He's never gone on for Sandy, and I hope to God he never does.

Gennaro at work in the seventies, still moving as effortlessly as he did in the fifties. In addition to his Broadway work, Peter produces and choreographs four to six spectacular stage shows at the Radio City Music Hall.

KODAK SAFETY FILM 5063 KODA

→25 →25A →26 →2

Martha Swope

We had to replace one of the orphans in the show, between Connecticut and rehearsal. It was apparent that she was becoming a young lady. We also wanted to add one child to the group of orphans. We had another casting call and saw one hundred and fifty more kids, from which two were selected. The adult company had to be supplemented as well. Three singers and dancers were added. At Goodspeed, there was a minimal amount of movement in the "dance" numbers because there wasn't enough room on the stage. For Broadway, we were opening up the musical from a dance standpoint.

Martha Swope

Martha Swope

In November we hired Peter Gennaro as the choreographer. His style, his speed, and his working ability with children would be beneficial to us. I was very happy to be working with Peter again. He was Jerome Robbins's co-choreographer on *West West Side Story* when I was a Jet, and Peter taught me how to do all the moves. Now, twenty years later, we were working together again.

An old friend of Charles's and mine was hired to be musical director. Peter Howard had done *Hello Dolly!, Mame, Here's Love, Carnival,* and many other Broadway shows.

In January, a week before we were scheduled to go into rehearsal, we were still shy $300,000. Meyer and Friedman had collected $250,000 from their investors and Nichols and Allen, $250,000 from theirs. It was then that Roger Stevens and the Kennedy Center and Jimmy Nederlander came to the rescue. The total capitalization occurred only two days before rehearsals started. We were now going to the Kennedy Center in Washington for an out-of-town opening in late February after five weeks of rehearsal in New York.

We had hired a very good press agent named David Powers, who had just been through the *Hellzapoppin* disaster. It was a million-and-a-half-dollar musical that closed out of town. Dave approached our property with the same apprehension everyone else originally had, but when he heard the show at a backers' audition, he fell in love too.

Rehearsals lasted five weeks at the Broadway Arts Studios. There was an air of anticipation about the project. You can tell when the word is out. There don't seem to

Jill Krementz

Peter Howard—the musical director is our surrogate in the pit. Performance to performance, he must be as consistent as a metronome and, at the same time, be sensitive to the subtle changes that occur onstage in order to maintain the internal tempo of the musical.

© Jill Krem

I wore two whistles around my neck during rehearsals— one could only be heard by children, the other by dogs.

be any problems. Nobody is getting fired after a week. The company is eager to come to rehearsal every day. The singers and dancers are not walking around complaining about the atmosphere. The general conditions and the work situation were good. The company came ready to work, eager to work. Little by little, I was able to pay attention to directing, to all of the details I was unable to get to in Connecticut. I began to shape and mold the musical from a characterization standpoint. Each day I would have four hours of rehearsal time with nothing to do but work with the children. Dorothy was working carefully to define the total character of Miss Hannigan. Reid was digging into the brittle new Warbucks that Tom had written into the story. The Connecticut cast had a head start on everybody else, but, as the group began to work together, the company was coming together as a company.

The unique thing about the *Annie* company, and I don't know the last time this happened historically, is that the same people who went out of town to Washington came back to New York. There was not a single replacement, a single firing, a single actor or member of the production staff who left the show. That's rare . . . very rare! There is often some moment of dissidence when an ego or a temper provokes a replacement. It did not happen with *Annie*. We stayed together. We were attached at the theatrical hip.

Word started to leak that there was a show in rehearsal *not* in trouble. Dave Powers's work began to pay off. The press was becoming interested in us. The first photograph appeared out of the blue. A Martha Swope picture of Reid, Andrea, and the dog was published in the *New York Times*. That photograph shocked everyone into recognition. Here were those one-dimensional cartoon characters fleshed out. Suddenly they were live beings, live people, live actors. That was the trigger for the beginning of the publicity that started before Washington.

Martha S

Laurie Beechman

Part of the fun of being in the *Annie* chorus
ensemble is the opportunity for each actor
to play four or more roles in the show.
The program tips the audience who are in on
the conceit from the beginning. They
accept and enjoy the wig and costume changes.
At the auditions, the actors read for
several parts and were hired without knowing
what roles they would play.

Donald Craig

Richard Ensslen

Meehan, Charnin, and Shelton, who may be hiding a Norelco nick

A woman named Gretchen Poston arrived at the rehearsal studio. She was Social Secretary to the White House, and had been working for the Carters for a month. She was also a friend of Roger Stevens and the Kennedy Center. Mrs. Poston had come to New York to audition *Annie* as the possible kick-off entertainment for the Carter Administration. It was the Governors' Dinner, at which President and Mrs. Carter would be entertaining the governors of the fifty states, justices of the Supreme Court, the Cabinet, and their wives. Mrs. Poston liked the segments she saw at the audition and asked us to do a twenty-five minute presentation at the Governors' Dinner on March 1.

We were apprehensive about opening in Washington because *Annie* is a musical with political overtones, and we were playing games with the New Deal. Roosevelt is a significant character in the show, and we were curious as to what the reaction to him would be. However, the Kennedy Center is such a gorgeous complex of theatres, the Eisenhower in particular, that we were willing to take the risk. From a financial standpoint, it made sense to go there, but we had a musical that didn't have a single well-known performer. We couldn't say in our publicity: "Come to see Mary Martin. Come to see Pearl Bailey. Come to see Carol Channing in a musical." We had one star to sell, and that was the show itself. That was *Annie*.

The advance ticket sales at the Kennedy Center were minimal—approximately $200,000 spread over a five-week period. We were, therefore, counting on good reviews. When you go out of town with no advance, it is very dangerous in terms of your future on Broadway, and, unless you get good reviews, you aren't going to have full houses. In the case of the Eisenhower, that means 1,100 people a night. We especially wanted full houses so we could get reactions and discover what to fix, what to change. Fifty people in a theatre reacting is not indicative of how to make fixes or changes, but 1,100 people a night is certainly the way you get your answer back.

Thomas Meehan never got paid enough when I asked him to work for me. On television, rumor has it that the money is good. Not so. Talent (on screen) gets the bucks and invariably you have to buy your writers a drink at Joe Allen's and look sad a lot and explain that you really want to do their sketch or their monologue but Gleason wants a fortune and where am I going to get the money and the sets cost an arm and a leg, and the next time I'll make it up to you, I promise, so call your agent and let me have this piece for a tenth of what it's worth, and besides that it'll be seen by thirty million people in one night and think about the fact that it'll make you famous, unquote.

Tom Meehan has heard this speech a lot. There were many drinks that I bought him in the last ten years as we worked together on television projects. It was, perhaps, this knowledge that made him a bit reluctant to become a Broadway debutant in 1972.

PHASES

1. You get the idea
2. You write down the idea
3. You finish writing the idea
4. You don't throw it out!
5. You audition what you haven't thrown out.
6. Somebody wants to produce the idea
7. The somebody actually raises the money.
8. You go into rehearsal
9. You stay in rehearsal
10. You go out-of-town
11. You open out-of-town
12. You don't close out of town
13. You do close out of town to come to New York
14. You load-in to a NY theatre
15. You play previews
16. You don't postpone your opening date.
17. You open
18. You get reviewed
19. You run or you close
20. Whether you run or you close — you get another idea!

When you are putting together a big musical, you have to deal with so many unknown quantities. Does the set fit inside the theatre? How do the moves work?

Is there enough time to make the costume changes? How do your actors make cross-overs? What does it really look like on a large stage? The Eisenhower proscenium opening is forty-one feet, double what the Goodspeed was. How would it look? How would the musical that was so confined in Connecticut translate itself to the Ike? There were many such questions on the way to Washington.

At this time, Tom and I were literally living together. Every night, we reviewed what we had done during the day. I told him there were twenty phases in a musical and invented a calendar of phases.

Annie was now at Phase Ten. We were working closely together, going over every line, every detail, every aspect of the musical. We were like convicts in a prison . . . crossing off the phases.

Rehearsals continued. In effect, the musical was finished just at the right time. We weren't in rehearsal too long. There was still enough work to be done, so that when the show went on in Washington the actors wouldn't lose their spontaneity. Washington held a couple of lasting memories for me. It had been the scene of some previous tryouts I had had, particularly the disastrous *Mata Hari* ten years earlier.

On Thursday night, February 24, we loaded out of New York. Tom, Laurie Beechman, and I took the last shuttle to Washington. It was a turbulent flight, and we were strapped in our seats and we were talking manically about everything except *Annie*.

At ten o'clock we walked from the hotel to the theatre. There it was, the John F. Kennedy Center for the Performing Arts, all lit up. The crew was loading in, and the next part of the adventure was upon us.

ACT II:
I Think I'm Gonna Like It Here

In 1973 Tom and Charles and I were pleading for a better time. The specific song that manifests the political mood of the authors is "Tomorrow," and the lyric was one of the first written for the show. The song was a reaction to what was going on in the country—the political situation, the war, the economy, the sense of quiet desperation that everyone had, the disenchantment with government leaders . . . there were no heroes. But the lyric says, "The sun'll come out tomorrow. Bet your bottom dollar that tomorrow there'll be sun," a very simple, naive statement. The end of the lyric says, "The sun'll come out tomorrow, so I gotta hang on till tomorrow, come what may. Tomorrow, tomorrow, I love ya, tomorrow. You're always a day away." That's the message of *Annie*. It is also correct in terms of the little girl. She is the eternal optimist . . . she is the light at the end of the tunnel . . . she's a person who stands there, chin up, facing all kinds of adversity. She will survive. We all want her to survive. We wanted the country to survive. That's why the song was written. That's why the song worked. That's why the show was written, because at the time when all the madness was going on Charles and Tom and I believed.

Martha Swope

OH, YOU'D KEEP MY SECRET, EH? HA! HA! THAT'S A GOOD ONE - WELL, YOU WON'T HAVE TO, PAL - I'LL KEEP IT --- WHAT? THEN YOU'LL KEEP THE TEN BILLION IN GEMS?

Harold Gray was an archconservative, and Oliver Warbucks was the equivalent of Ronald Reagan today. We didn't agree with Gray's interpretation of Warbucks. That was the confusion. We had to get our house in order in terms of our attitude toward Warbucks. We wrote the story of a man who believed in his country. A man who was—as far as Gray was concerned—anti-Roosevelt. We perceived of him as a realist. When Roosevelt became President, Warbucks realized he had to work with him in order to survive. That is, in essence, what manifests itself on the stage of the Alvin Theatre. Warbucks and Roosevelt are strange bedfellows, their relationship works because they respect each other and work together to make things happen. They have faith and courage. In the play, Warbucks believes in the country and in the economy, and he triggers the New Deal when he brings Annie to Washington. Roosevelt, in effect, pays Annie back for the New Deal by eventually giving Warbucks assistance with J. Edgar Hoover, the head of the F.B.I., in the search for Annie's parents.

Martha Swope

Reid cared. From day-one he was a conscientious and dedicated crafts-
man who tried all of the changes that were thrown at him with great
courage. There were often times when he rehearsed a new Warbucks
in the afternoon and played an old Warbucks at night. I hope,
when all this is over, his hair grows back.

Ted Azar, the *Annie* hair stylist, taking care of a last-minute touch up

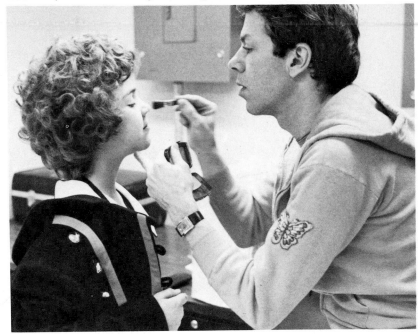

© Jill Krementz

In Washington, during the loading time, when we were trying to see
whether the set fit in the theatre, to figure out the moves, to put the costumes
together, to get the makeup done right, and to work out the orchestra, I was also
organizing an evening's entertainment for the White House.

Martha Swope

The "Tomorrow" reprise in the Cabinet scene. A portion of this scene
and number was performed in the miniature version of *Annie* at the White House.
President Carter told us later he had chosen his cabinet too early.

March 1 was not only the night of the Governors' Dinner, but it was our first
preview. We couldn't figure how we were going to be in two places at the same time.
The first thing we did was to schedule the preview performance a half hour earlier,
and to arrange the White House show for a half hour later to give us time to move
the cast from the Kennedy Center to the White House.

Tom, Charles, and I had prepared a twenty-five-minute condensation of the script. We
had a ten o'clock run-through in the East Room of the White House for photographers
and news media. We were going to be on television the next day, and the only time
the press would be allowed to photograph would be at our White House rehearsal. That
morning we trooped the entire company—twenty-seven actors, the stage manager,
Charles, and Peter Howard, the musical director—over in a chartered bus from the
Kennedy Center, making sure Sandy did what he had to do outside on the grounds.

We rehearsed at the Kennedy Center later, and that night saw the musical in
front of an audience for the first time. It was thrilling. Dorothy was brilliant. Reid
was wonderful (it was good that he was bald). Andrea sang her heart out. The
audience responded to the jokes. They bought F.D.R. and the fun we were having
with the Cabinet. They loved the new number we had written, "We'd Like to Thank
You Herbert Hoover," the satirical lyric that thanked the ex-President for putting the
country in the condition it was in. The audience was warm and supportive and
stood up at the end of the play. It was a standing ovation in Washington on a preview
night! Everyone jumped with joy, but we didn't have time to savor the moment.

As soon as the curtain call was over, we were rushed onto a bus and driven to the White House, where they fed the kids milk and cookies and gave us coffee. As we listened to the Marine Band accompanying the guests into the East Room, we did a verbal brushup of our mini-show. The call to be ready was given. The President of the United States introduced us to the assembly. The music was provided by two pianos in the ballroom: Peter was at one and Charles was at the other; he was playing on the Nixon-Truman piano. I stood like an anxious father in the back of the room, directly next to Governor Hugh Carey of New York. On the other side stood Gretchen Poston who was nervous too because it was her debut as a producer for the Carters.

Edwin Bordo—
the butler loses
his cool

Martha Swope

The orphans getting
ready to perform
"You're Never Fully
Dressed Without a Smile"

The servants and Annie,
when she arrives
at the Warbucks mansion

The President and Mrs. Carter
welcome the Governors of the
States and Territories
to an evening at The White House

March 1, 1977

Mr. Peter Duchin
at the
Piano

DINNER

Meir's
Ohio State
Sherry

Clear Beef Broth
Cheese Twists

Mirassou
California
Gamay
Beaujolais

Roast Duckling
with Orange Sauce
Wild Rice
Buttered Brussels Sprouts

Great Western
New York State
Champagne

Bibb Lettuce Salad
Trappist Cheese

Wild Blackberry Chiffon Pie

Demitasse

A New Musical

THE JOHN F. KENNEDY CENTER FOR THE PERFORMING ARTS
and
MIKE NICHOLS
Present
Annie

Book by
IRWIN MEYER   STEPHEN R. FRIEDMAN   LEWIS ALLEN

...AS MEEHAN   CHARLES STROUSE   MARTIN CHARNIN

ANDREA   REID
McARDLE   SHELTON
SANDY   ROBERT
FAISON   FITCH

DOROTHY LOUDON

RAYMOND THORNE   LAURIE BEECHMAN

DAVID MITCHELL   THEONI V. ALDREDGE   JUDY RASMUSON

PETER HOWARD   PHILIP J. LANG   JANET BEROZA

PETER GENNARO

MARTIN CHARNIN

Based on "LITTLE ORPHAN ANNIE"
By Permission of Chicago Tribune – New York News Syndicate, Inc.

MICHAEL P. PRICE, Executive Producer

...ening's entertainment...

Leapin' Lizards! Whatever happened to "Little Orphan Annie"?

The preposterous rumor that she turned into a new musical produced by Mike Nichols
and came to the White House to welcome our nations' governors turns out to be true.

"Annie" brings with her Oliver Warbucks, the richest man in the world, her dog
Sandy who, as everyone knows, says "Arf", and some other characters from the early
1930s who will be exquisitely familiar.

The distinguished guests reacted similarly to the way the audience had reacted at the theatre earlier. President Carter stood up. We got a second standing ovation, this time including the President of the United States. The most thrilling and emotional moment was at the end when the entire company sang "Tomorrow." Governor George Wallace began singing "Tomorrow" as though he knew the song, with tears streaming down his face, particularly at the point where the lyrics went, "Tomorrow. So I gotta hang on till tomorrow, come what may! Tomorrow, tomorrow, I love ya tomorrow. You're always a day away."

We received a wonderful reception on every level that night. Completely exhausted, we piled back in the bus and were deposited at our hotels. Tom and I spent the night going over what had to be done the next day. There were scenes that were thick, that needed cutting. Charles and I had agreed that the musical changes would be made later on. Some book problems had to be solved first, and some technical aspects had to be attended to because the set was monumental. The work continued throughout the week.

The White House Photographer

Mrs. Poston ingeniously combined our theatre poster with her menu as a souvenir for each guest, and generously printed an extra hundred for the *Annie* company and crew.

For Martin Charnin,

with thanks —

Jimmy Carter   Rosalynn Carter

The word-of-mouth had begun, and ticket sales were building. We opened to a full house on Saturday night. The reviews were published Monday morning, and we got nine raves—the kind of reviews that mothers write for their children.

Monday morning, the telephones at the Kennedy Center blew out. At ten o'clock Tuesday during rehearsal, Janet Beroza, the production stage manager, handed me a note: the entire run had gone clean by ten o'clock. Sold out. Completely sold out. From then on, the only way to get a seat was to get in line at eight o'clock in the morning and wait for standing room. Additional groups of lines would queue up at seven-thirty at night to see if there were cancellations.

We went clean for the whole run, and played thirty-two performances—four weeks, eight performances a week—during which we received thirty-two standing ovations. It was phenomenal, absolutely phenomenal.

We became very "in." The second the public can't get tickets to a show, the people associated with it become celebrities. We were the pets of the city. If you said you were with *Annie* you could get a table at a restaurant, you would get room service faster. If you had anything to do with the show, you were a hero. It was a

---

luxurious four weeks in Washington. The press was very good to us. Three times a week, there was a column item, some piece of publicity attached to the show—an interview with Andrea, with Dorothy, with Reid, with Charles, Tom and myself.

In March the announcement ad for *Annie* went into the *New York Times*. We called to find out what the response was. The word had, indeed, traveled to New York.

At the same time that we were delighted with our success, we were not seduced into believing we were finished. Washington, in its last season, had given enthusiastic reviews to two shows that came to New York and didn't make it. One was *Texas Trilogy,* the other was a musical called *Music Is. Texas Trilogy* ran about two months, and *Music Is* closed in about a week.

We still had work to do. Technical problems with the timing and staging had to be solved. "N.Y.C." still wasn't working as a number. It was too thick and didn't have a total focus. We never stopped making improvements, which is what you have to do to make an out-of-town hit a New York hit. You can't rest on your laurels and believe that because the critics and the audiences are going bananas over you that your work is done.

Queueing up for standing room after the Washington reviews

Richard Braat

MAIL ORDERS ACCEPTED NOW!

Annie

A New Musical

MIKE NICHOLS
Presents

Annie

Produced by
IRWIN MEYER STEPHEN R. FRIEDMAN LEWIS ALLEN

Book by   Music by   Lyrics by
THOMAS MEEHAN CHARLES STROUSE MARTIN CHARNIN

Starring

ANDREA   REID
McARDLE   SHELTON

SANDY   ROBERT
FAISON   FITCH

and

DOROTHY LOUDON

With

RAYMOND THORNE   LAURIE BEECHMAN

Settings by   Costumes by   Lighting by
DAVID MITCHELL   THEONI V. ALDREDGE   JUDY RASMUSON

Musical Direction and   Orchestrations   Production
Dance Music Arranged by   by   Stage Manager
PETER HOWARD   PHILIP J. LANG   JANET BEROZA

Musical Numbers Choreographed by

PETER GENNARO

Entire Production Directed by

MARTIN CHARNIN

Based on LITTLE ORPHAN ANNIE ®
by Permission of Chicago Tribune · New York News Syndicate, Inc.
Produced in Association with PETER CRANE
Originally Produced by the Goodspeed Opera House
MICHAEL P. PRICE, Executive Producer

PREVIEWS BEGIN WED. EVG. APRIL 6 thru WED. EVG. APRIL 20
OPENS THURSDAY EVENING, APRIL 21

Tues. thru Fri. Evgs. at 8 P.M., Sat.Mat. at 2 P.M. & Sun. Mat. at 3 P.M.: Orch. & Mezz.; $16.50; Balc.; $15, 13, 10, 8.
Sat. Evg. at 8 P.M.: Orch. & Mezz.; $17.50; Balc.; $15, 12, 11, 9. Wed. Mat. at 2 P.M.;Orch. & Mezz.; $14; Balc. $12, 10, 9, 8.
Please enclose a self-addressed,stamped envelope and list alternate dates.

FOR GROUP SALES CALL: (212)354-1032
(212) 575-5056

ALVIN THEATRE, 250 W. 52nd St.,N.Y., N.Y. 10019
"SHENANDOAH" MOVES MARCH 29 to MARK HELLINGER THEATRE

The first ad that appeared in the *New York Times*. It's the one you wait for—
the one that has the most emotional impact. We hung it on the wall of
the Green Room at the Eisenhower for everyone to see.

One of the things you have to prepare for is middle-of-the-road reviews on Broadway. If you get them, and you don't have enough money to advertise, then you're in trouble. So a healthy chunk of money should be allotted for television advertising, radio spots, print ads. An ad in the *New York Times* on Sunday costs $17,500, not including the production costs. Many shows have $17,500 as their entire advertising budget.

Richard Braaten

Ten A.M. and the line is still going strong.
On the right is Peter Neufeld, who is half of our
general manager team; Tyler Gatchel is the other.

One of the reasons that I love working in the theatre is the constant gratification you get from performance to performance. You work very hard on a television show, but when it goes on the air at nine o'clock, it becomes molecules; it disappears. In a strange way it's the same with a film. Once you cut a film and release it, the audience sees it and reacts, but you can't go back and redo any of the work. The theatre is the only structured medium that allows you the luxury of this interaction with the audience. Every night X number of people give you an answer . . . they applaud, they cheer, they boo, they hiss, they react. It's a continuous living experience for the two and a half hours you are in the theatre. You have to pay attention to your audiences. You listen for their silence . . . their coughing . . . their tears . . . their gasps. You become very skilled in listening for a laugh, where it is coming from, and why. Once you have mastered the craft of listening, you begin to get rid of the small laughs, to go for the big ones. You get rid of all the moments that provoke uncomfortable silences, that diffuse the emotional line of the play. It is not like reading a book. You can't turn the pages back and reread a passage to decide what the author meant. You have to make sure that every time you say something in the theatre, you mean it and it is understood. It is probably the most intentional medium there is. We were constantly listening to the give of the show and the take of the audience . . . and then the return. It's a give−take−give situation.

The audience has an enormous impact on the performers. A bad audience intimidates them, and sometimes they overcompensate for a lack of attention by pushing too hard. The further an actor pushes, the further away he is pushing the audience. The safest thing to do is to pull back and draw the audience closer to you.

There was an important moment, for example, in the second act of *Annie* when we didn't want the audience to react incorrectly to a very emotional line of dialogue. There was a danger that they might. The way it was solved was to have the actor say the line very quietly, so that the audience, as a unit, had to crane its neck just that inch to listen to what the actor was saying.

In Connecticut, we had written a song for Warbucks's secretary about her unrequited feelings for him. It was a very honest, honorable moment on the stage. Sandy Faison sang it beautifully. The orchestration was terrific. At that particular moment in the play, however, the audience didn't care. What they cared about was whether Annie was going to find her parents, and whether Warbucks and Annie were going to get together. After three weeks, the audience told us, by being restless, that they wanted us to get on with it, to tell the crucial part of the story. The song went. It was difficult to tell Sandy that the song had to be cut, but she understood why. Actors aren't fools. They know when they are holding something up, even though

Sandy Faison, who brought
a bit of Carole Lombard
to the role of Warbucks's
secretary—a tireless
worker and a good friend.

their egos are being gratified when the spotlight belongs to them. If an actor shines in a play that doesn't shine, the actor is not going to be in that play very long. It's a community effort. A wonderful score and no book will not make a hit musical . . . a wonderful book and no score will not make it either. All of these things have equal weight in the making of a success.

Rosalyn Carter backstage with the orphans.
She invited the children to the White House to
play with Amy. Danielle, once there, went
looking for Harold Ickes and Cordell Hull.

"Would the company please stay on stage,
there are some celebrities in the house who
would like to come and say hello to you."

Not a week passed without at least five
star-studded performances. Henry Fonda
came to see us. Liv Ullmann, who was in *Anna
Christie* at the National Theatre, came to
see us. Ex-President Ford . . . Dr. Kissinger
. . . Vice-President and Mrs. Mondale
. . . the Japanese Ambassador. . . the
Speaker of the House . . . Mrs. Carter . . .
Amy came to see us twice. It was like meeting
the queen every night after the show. And
there was a genuine sense of joy and love. You
can tell it is more than just a lip-service visit
when you hear, "You were wonderful, terrific,
and thank you very much for being in our theatre." The Washingtonians came back and
were generous and excited and sincere about
their feelings for the play and the performers.
They also ran—they raced—to have their pictures taken with the dog. Sandy became a major celebrity in Washington.

His Excellency Fumihiko Togo and Mrs. Togo, Embassy of Japan

FINALE: N.Y.C.

The anticipation of New York began to creep into every performance. We were all shooting for that opening on Broadway. While we were in Washington, the news of our success filtered into New York, and the New Yorkers began to appear. Our friends came down with mixed feelings. They came with disbelief; the show couldn't be as good as everyone said. And often the disbelievers went away saying, "My goodness, it really works!"

We closed in Washington in April and began loading into the Alvin Theatre in New York over the weekend. The theatre holds memories for me because *West Side Story* had played there some eighteen years before. I returned to the Alvin Theatre this time, not as a performer or a paying customer, but as the director of this enormous musical called *Annie*. I was reunited with a stage crew I had literally not seen in all of that time, but who looked as familiar as they had on the last day of the *West Side* run. They remembered me, and it was a joyful, friendly meeting.

After our arrival, it took four days of loading in before our first preview on Friday night. Then we were to play eighteen previews prior to the opening on April 21.

On the night of the first preview, a very hard audience came to see the show. They came with their noses in the air, firmly convinced it was just another Washington mistake. How could it be as good as Washington had said it was? It was still Little Orphan Annie, and who cared about it? New York preview audiences are notoriously difficult. They are smart, tough, sophisticated theatre-goers.

The Etheredges

When that first preview
audience was on its feet cheering
at the end of the performance,
I felt we were home.

The improvements did not stop,
however. As much time as you program and
assign to the work, it is still difficult to
accomplish everything. Certain things were
left for my decision, were left to the end—
things that I couldn't attend to in
Washington, in rehearsals or on the stage. I
had to wait to do them in New York.

"Easy Street" was written in Connecticut to replace a song called "That's the Way It Goes," which went. Charles and I were working on this new number during a hectic restaging period and I was dividing my time between the piano room and the rehearsal hall. During a lunch break, the cleaning man threw away the unfinished lyric and music, and we spent four hours going through the garbage to find it.

Martha Swope

Martha Swope

Martha Swope

The last musical number to be solved was "N.Y.C." We worked on it through the previews in New York, changing it, reorchestrating it, reshaping it, restaging it, reshifting it, writing new lyrics for it. We were very aware that we were doing a Valentine to New York City and were worried about singing the praise of New York in New York. Many great songs had preceded us.

The work circumstance in New York is different from Washington. You are now on a different contract with Actors' Equity, because you're no longer on the road. You are previewing in New York, and rehearsal hours change drastically. In Washington we had a five- or six-hour call with three hours of performance each day, but in New York, we had only three hours of work plus the performance; we lost two hours. I relentlessly zeroed in on what had to be done. The pressure was gigantic for all of us.

All photographs in the color section by Martha Swope

It's the Hard-Knock Life

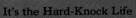
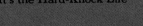

We'd Like to Thank You Herbert Hoover

Easy Street

Tomorrow (Reprise)

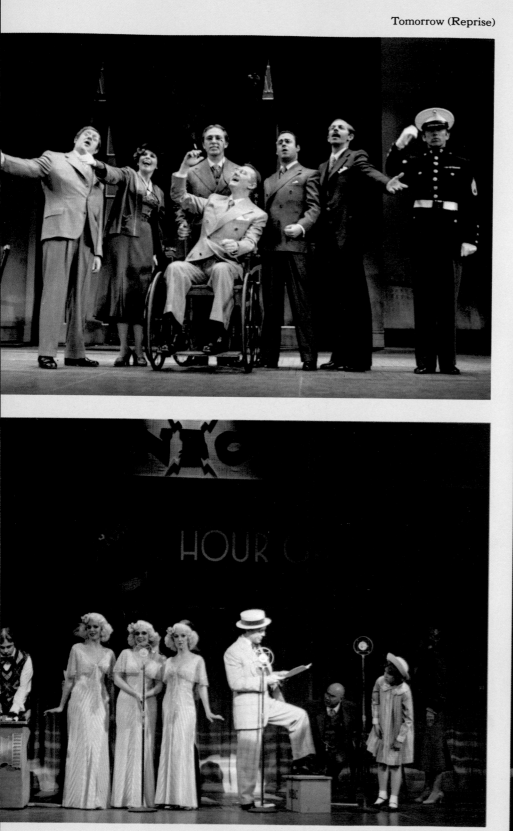

N.Y.C.

A New Deal for Christmas

You're Never Fully Dressed Without a Smile

I Don't Need
Anything But You

RICHFIELD

Martha Swope

There was no time to sleep. We performed, we rehearsed. There were a thousand details involving the set, re-dressing certain aspects of the show, checking sound balances in the orchestra pit. The sound was different at the Alvin from what it was Kennedy Center . . . the sight lines were different . . . the space backstage was different . . . the dressing rooms were different . . . *everything* was different.

Everyone had to straighten out his own department, but the final approval is given by the director. It all comes to me. I am right smack in the middle. My adrenalin is working double time. I had to make instant decisions and I had to live with them. If they didn't work, I had to try something else.

The director is constantly having meetings, and listening to the choreographer's notes about spacing, to the musical director's notes, the composer's notes, the book writer's notes. Also, my friends were coming to the theatre saying, "Listen, it's terrific, but if you only shifted this to that and this to there, boy, it would really be 150 percent better." You are like a sieve, trying to keep the information you think is necessary and valuable and let the rest of it go through you. The last couple of weeks are wildly pressure-packed. Every day that goes by is a day closer to that terrifying moment when the *New York Times,* the *New York Post,* and the *Daily News* are

going to say yes or no. But, you try not to think about the reviews. I didn't have time to think about them anyway. The advertising campaign had to be dealt with. The quote ads had to be planned. If we got good reviews, how would they be excerpted? What was the advertising campaign going to be on radio? On television? I had to be in twenty-five different places at the same time. The days were very long, but not long enough.

On top of everything else, we were being assaulted from every direction by the media, who believed Washington. The day after we returned from Washington, we went to Richard Avedon's studio for the first of many super-publicity sessions. Leo Lerman, the critic for *Vogue* and author of the "People Are Talking About" column was there and did the first New York interview. In April *Vogue* was committing itself to a story to be released in June. We knew the editors believed we were going to be around for a while.

Appeared in April 17, 1977 *New York Times*. Drawing courtesy The Margo Feiden Galleries, New York City

It's these little hints that let you know you may have a hit. We heard that Al Hirschfeld had been in Washington the week before we closed to do a cartoon for the *New York Times*. The morning we got back to New York we learned that Hirschfeld had loved the show and was planning to do the biggest caricature he had done since *Fiddler*—a six-column cartoon across the top of the Sunday *New York Times*. At one of our rehearsals, Sam Norkin arrived to do his cartoon for the New York *Daily News*.

Then the pre-opening interviews started with the *Village Voice*, *Newsweek*, *People*, *New York*. All of this was going on simultaneously with our efforts to fine tune the show.

Fifty-second Street welcomed us with open kitchens. We were helping business on the street. Gallagher's Restaurant was packed. Jilly's was packed. Los Madriles, an Argentinian restaurant, had just opened down the street and they were looking for business. When the lines began to form at the Alvin Theatre, Los Madriles also believed its year was made.

On April 19, I froze the show—the last work was done. The actors played the next three performances without a change. I had requested that the producers allow the critics to see the play over three performances so that the pressure of a single viewing would be taken off the actors. The producers agreed. Clive Barnes, the *New York Times* critic, had decided to come to the Wednesday matinee; three critics were coming Wednesday night; and the balance would be there on our official opening night, Thursday, April 21.

To be honest, opening nights are terrible because the audience is filled with investors and friends, who overreact. They love everything, and that infuriates the critics. Barnes came to a matinee with civilians in the audience and got a taste of exactly how the show affected a general audience; he saw a very good performance. The critics who came Wednesday night also saw a good performance, because it was again a civilian house.

Mike Nichols made a terrific decision with regard to the opening night performance. The company and production personnel could have as many tickets as they wanted for their friends, but the one requirement was that the audience had to be fresh. No one could come who had already seen the show. We couldn't have people there who knew what to expect, who knew where the laughs were.

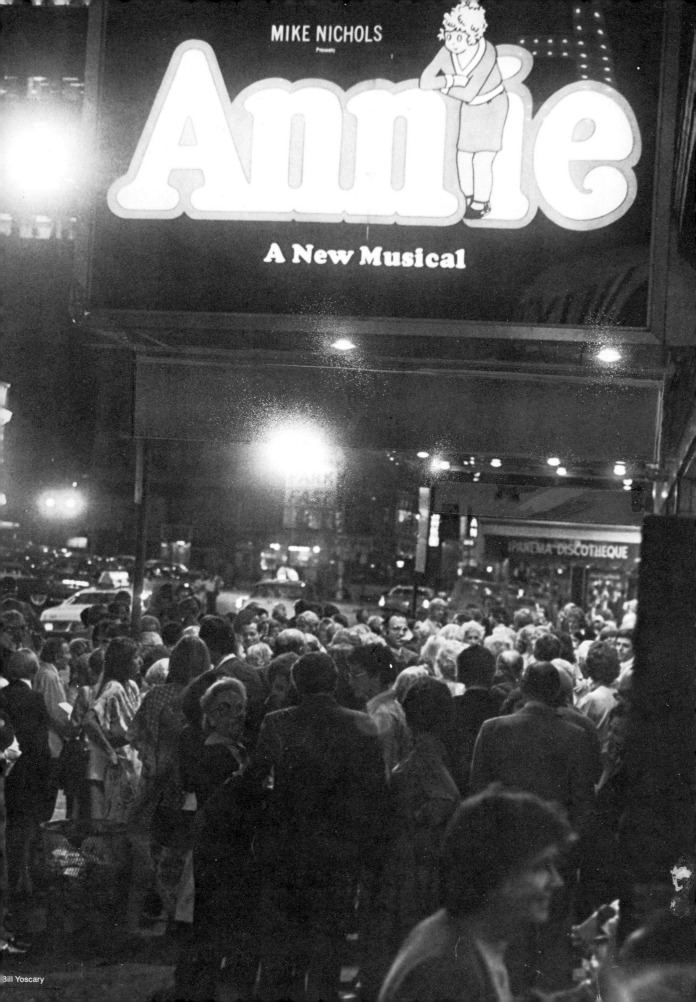

There is nothing like opening night in New York. The electricity, the excitement, the glamour, the fear, the noise. It all comes with a rush. People that you have been living with for six years, look at you as though they have no idea who you are. Their eyes glaze over. It's hectic and crazy and wonderful. Charles Strouse has historically never gone to an opening night. I think on opening night of *Bye Bye Birdie* he locked himself in a broom closet in the basement of the Shubert Theatre and spent the entire show listening through the cracks in the wall. That night Charles felt confident enough to sit in the orchestra. Tom Meehan must have smoked fifty cigarettes. There was a cloud in the back of the house, and if the fire commissioner had been there, we would have all been locked up. I paced. I stood in the back of the theatre and I walked. I don't think I was in one spot for more than thirty seconds. I watched it . . . I didn't watch it. It was totally out of my hands. My ears had become so accustomed to the audience's reaction that I could hear the slightest difference, whether the laughs were bigger or smaller . . . .

It was a positively glorious opening, with a lot of celebrities in the audience: Julie Styne, Alan Jay Lerner, Lynn Redgrave, Alan Bates, Paul Simon, Shelly Duvall, Hermione Gingold, Beatrice Straight, Claudette Colbert, Candice Bergen, Lillian Hellman.

It was good. It was as simple as that.

Bill Yoscary

OH! WHAT WILL THE CRITICS SAY?

HAROLD GRAY

Opening night presents can be a source for a lot of fun. On April 21 the *Annie* company, orchestra, production staff, and stage crew got silver "Annies" I had had designed and executed by a silversmith friend in Washington. Charles got a photo blow-up of an original part of the Gray comic strip, doctored to list all the musical numbers cut out of the show since its inception. Mike, who spent the last three preview performances next to me in the back of the house tapping me on the shoulder every time he felt the actors were taking too many pauses, got a Mason jar filled with blank strips of paper identified as "all of the pauses cut out of the show in previews." Tom got a plaque—one that looked like something you might find in the office of the owner of the Yankees or the Mets. It was an Honor Roll—eighty names on little brass plates. The inscription read:

The following characters have given their lives in the service of Thomas E. Meehan

On each plaque was the name of a character that had been cut out of the musical.

During intermission there were a lot of hugs and kisses and congratulations. Everyone was smiling. When the curtain came down, the audience was standing up and cheering. There were a lot of curtain calls. Andrea got an incredible reaction . . . Dorothy just locked it up . . . they loved Reid. They loved everybody. Sandy got an enormous hand for doing his six tricks.

The producers had decided they were going to throw a big bash, a big opening night party at Gallagher's Restaurant. It was the biggest opening night party on Broadway since *Fiddler.* Everyone was convinced he had seen a hit. I've been at opening night parties where a pall is cast very early. People sense it when a show is not going to survive; there is a false joy that permeates the room. But that night there was a lot of eating, drinking and dancing and fun—you can't invent that kind of fun on opening night.

Martha Swope

We had hired an orchestra. They were playing Rodgers and Hammerstein, Cole Porter, and Strouse! They were playing "N.Y.C." and "I Don't Need Anything but You" and "Tomorrow," and we were dancing to our music.

At eleven o'clock while the party was going on, Charles, Tom, and I went to the advertising agency where three television sets were running simultaneously. We heard the first reviews on WCBS with Pat Collins, Bob Lape on WABC, and Pia Lindstrom on WNBC. Pat Collins couldn't have been more glowing. On her one-to-ten scale, we got nine. We read Barnes's review next, and it was a rave. Bob Lape said this, William Raidy said that, and at this point when you listen to reviews you don't hear them or read them. You look for quotes—the kind of catch-phrases you know will end up on your billboards. We were hearing the words: ". . . run forever," ". . . a boon to mankind," ". . . an incredible achievement." There were dissenters; there were people who didn't like the show. But, at that moment in time, it didn't matter.

The next morning, the morning of the twenty-second, the phones at the Alvin Theatre were blowing out. There were seventy-five people on the ticket line. We knew we had a major hit. The size of it was not apparent until a week later, when they had to install seven new telephone lines in the box office, when the mail increased, when the American Express charges increased. *Annie* was racking up twenty to thirty thousand dollars a day. *Annie* had arrived.

During the six years from Christmas 1971 to April 1977, I pulled "Little Orphan Annie" inch by inch toward that Broadway opening. It was imperative to get *Annie* on. In the dark hours, I just wanted to see it live. I always believed it would be what it has become. Originally, there were not a lot of people who believed with me. Tom and Charles were first. Slowly but surely, others believed too—Jane Chodorov, who was my agent at William Morris; Agnes Kelliher, who ran the New York office of E.H. Morris; E. H. himself; David Cogan, my business manager; Jack Lemmon, Jerry Stiller and Anne Meara, Carol Hall, Bill and Arlene Gerber, Elliott Lawrence, Elliot Tozer, Tom Geoly, Mike and Ed Gifford, Yvette Schumer, and Joe Allen, who each loaned me a thousand dollars in 1974 so I could maintain the payment of the rights; Janice Steele, my production assistant who put up with *some* of my nonsense; Sylvia Pancotti, my production assistant who put up with *all* of my nonsense; and Dick Ticktin, my attorney since 1974, who may *yet* get paid for all the work he's done.

I invested all the money that I had, all the money that I had made, in helping to keep *Annie* afloat, in paying for the rights and keeping the rights going over the six-year period. Many contracts were signed, and lawyers, telephone calls, postage, etc. were needed. Money was being spent constantly, and I spent the last $2,000 that I had in the world on opening-night presents for some seventy people in the show. I left myself 60 cents on April 21—20 cents for the *New York Times;* 15 cents for the *Daily News;* and 25 cents for the *New York Post,* because that was where it was at. Those three papers were going to give us the answer.

Telegram

IA323(2104)(1-022657A111)PD 04/21/77 2103

DEAR MARTY
JUST MY LUCK A RED HEAD NAMED ANNIE AND IM TOO
OLD FOR THE PART TSKTTSK
HAVE A GREAT OPENING
    ANN MARGARET

MMM

western union Mailgram

2-053471E110 04/20/77 ICS IPMMTZZ CSP NYAC
  2023388730 MGM TDMT WASHINGTON DC 100 04-20 0649P EST

I received over six hundred wires and notes and gifts on opening night. There were fifty-five wires that used "tenacious" or "tenacity." Western Union learned how to spell "tenacity" on April 21, 1977.

My favorite telegram came from Alan Jay Lerner: WELL KID, YOU SURE DID IT THIS TIME. IT'LL RUN FOREVER AND IT'S YOUR SHOW AND I COULDN'T BE HAPPIER. CONGRATULATIONS, I'LL FORGIVE YOU THIS TIME BUT DON'T DO IT AGAIN!

Charles Strouse got a lovely wire from Stuart Ostrow, the producer of *Pippin:* I SAW ANNIE IN PREVIEWS LAST WEEK AND I CRIED TWICE. ONCE WHEN ANNIE SINGS 'MAYBE,' AND THEN AGAIN AT THE END OF THE SHOW WHEN THE CURTAIN CAME DOWN AND I REALIZED I WASN'T THE PRODUCER.

---

850 7 AVE
NEWYORK NY 10019

RICHARD L COE
2713 DUMBARTON NORTHWEST
WASHINGTON DC 20007

western union Mailgram

2-053471E110 04/20/77 ICS IPMMTZZ CSP NYAC
  2023388730 MGM TDMT WASHINGTON DC 100 04-20 0649P EST

ALOST ON MY PRAYER RUG BUT THINKING OF YOU ALL WITH HIGH CONFIDENCES
ARF ARF

DICK COE

18:50 EST

I threw a party to celebrate our 100th performance on Broadway.
The concept of parties began in Connecticut, when every birthday was celebrated.
The practice has and will continue, I suspect for the life of the show.
Everybody shows up…

Tom, Charles, and I have maintained a wonderful working relationship over the course of these six years. Our lives have changed radically—*Annie* has become important to the American Musical Theatre. We laugh a lot. We are enjoying our success, and enjoying the pleasure that *Annie* has brought to the American public. There is nothing more thrilling than watching the audience stream out of the Alvin Theatre with a happy glow, and it happens consistently.

Everybody

CURTAIN CALL: Tomorrow

One of the great luxuries of having a hit show is that all the money you tucked away for advertising can now be taken out of the budget because advertising becomes publicity when you have a hit. The press starts calling you. It's also lunacy to advertise something you can't get tickets to. Our original budget allowed for a campaign that would go a year and a half. Now we only pay for our theatrical listings. When the awards started coming in, however, the show was publicized.

After opening night, the free publicity began. The *New York Times* was there, the *Post* was there, the *Daily News* was there. The "Today" show was there. The magazines were there. Our review in *Newsweek* was three pages long; we were in the fashion section of the *Times*, in the theatre section of the *Times*. Everything was *Annie, Annie, Annie*. Earl Wilson was carrying a story about us every single day. So was Liz Smith in the *Daily News*. We were hot copy. Andrea was important, Dorothy was important, Reid was important . . . the *show* was important. The fact that we were a great boost to the economy of New York City was important; and that we were a musical in the truest sense of the word was important.

My colleagues in show business were enthusiastic about the musical, genuinely so. The Jerry Hermans and Alan Jay Lerners and Richard Rodgers of the world were saying not only, "Congratulations," but, "Thank you, thank you, because you made it possible for us to go back to work again. You brought the musical theatre back. You brought the musical comedy back."

Walter Kerr came on the opening night. His review didn't print for two weeks because he writes as a Sunday critic rather than a daily critic. Walter Kerr was the one reviewer that Tom, Charles, and I wanted to turn around more than anyone else. The following notice appears every Sunday in the "Arts and Leisure Guide" in the *New York Times:*

Broadway

ANNIE—The Tony Award musical inspired by the comic strip "Little Orphan Annie," in which Annie becomes the symbol of the Great Depression and Franklin D. Roosevelt's New Deal. Book by Thomas Meehan, music by Charles Strouse, lyrics by Martin Charnin, who also is director. Andrea McArdle, Reid Shelton and Dorothy Loudon star. "An old legend is made into a new one, ... We're forthrightly invited to lose our minds at the Alvin, and that—reluctantly at first, then helplessly—is what we do." (Kerr) Alvin, 250 W. 52d St. (PL 7-8646)

BEATLEMANIA—A two-hour half-concert, half-theatrical event that blends a sequence of Beatles songs played by imitation Beatles, with a slide show depicting events of the 1960's. "An ingratiating enough affair, if you don't take it too seriously." (Rockwell) Winter Garden, 1634 Bway, at 50th St. (CI 5-4878)

BUBBLING BROWN SUGAR—A revue which purports to be a musical history of Harlem. Clive Barnes thought the music "most likable and lovable," the

One of the interested parties in the fortunes of *Annie* is the Chicago Tribune-New York News Syndicate, which published the original "Little Orphan Annie" comic strip. In the first negotiations in 1971 to secure the rights, part of the agreement was that they had approval of the first draft of the script and, as underlying rights owners, they were always kept abreast of our intentions. Robert Reed, president of the Syndicate, was made aware of the fact we were changing and shifting characters in order to accommodate the needs of our musical, and he gave us total support.

We have revitalized the name Annie. In 1975, "Little Orphan Annie" had been taken out of some of the major newspapers. The comic strip is still being syndicated in many places, but she is an entirely new phenomenon now, as far as they are concerned. The rights have merged—"Little Orphan Annie," the comic strip, and *Annie,* the musical, are now synonymous. From a merchandising point of view, everything belongs to the same base.

The merchandising of this kind of event is comparable to what happened only one time before in the history of the theatre—when Snoopy and Charlie Brown became so successful. There are any number of ancillary things that can happen on a Broadway show, but, with *Annie,* the field is wide open. There will be *Annie* jewelry . . . *Annie* toys . . . *Annie* patterns for dresses . . . *Annie* lockets . . . *Annie* towels . . . *Annie* T-shirts, and we are being very scrupulous about who will be allowed to do the merchandising. The national companies will go out in 1978, when they will begin to hit all of the major cities in the United States. After touring, one company will go to Chicago and another to Los Angeles for open-end engagements. Now, of course, the motion picture studios are pressuring us to make a motion picture deal. The movie will be made, but it will not compete with the play.

Gene Shalit and our gang at the "Today Show"

Bill Kean

Janet Beroza

Diana Barrows, Drew Murphy,
our company manager,
and Jim Hosbein

The investors have started getting their money back. They have already received distributions. It will take about thirty weeks to pay off this show, after which the investor will begin to make his profits.

My attorney keeps reminding me, "You don't have problems when you have a flop. You only have problems when you have a hit." But they're wonderful problems to have. You find yourself trying to determine what the right moves are, what the right deals are. You try very hard to maintain the show's profile, its attitude, its class.

Krementz

© Jill Krementz

The original cast album was recorded by Columbia Records one week after we opened on Broadway. The score wouldn't fit on a single disc and cuts had to be made. We reduced the score to forty-five minutes of music; the session took twelve hours. Minor adjustments were made in the orchestration to accommodate the larger band. The album was released three weeks later—one record store in New York had a sign in its window that simply said, "IT'S HERE." At the recording session the regulars with Don Ellis, executive producer of the album (left, front) and Larry Morton (right, front), who co-produced the album with Charles.

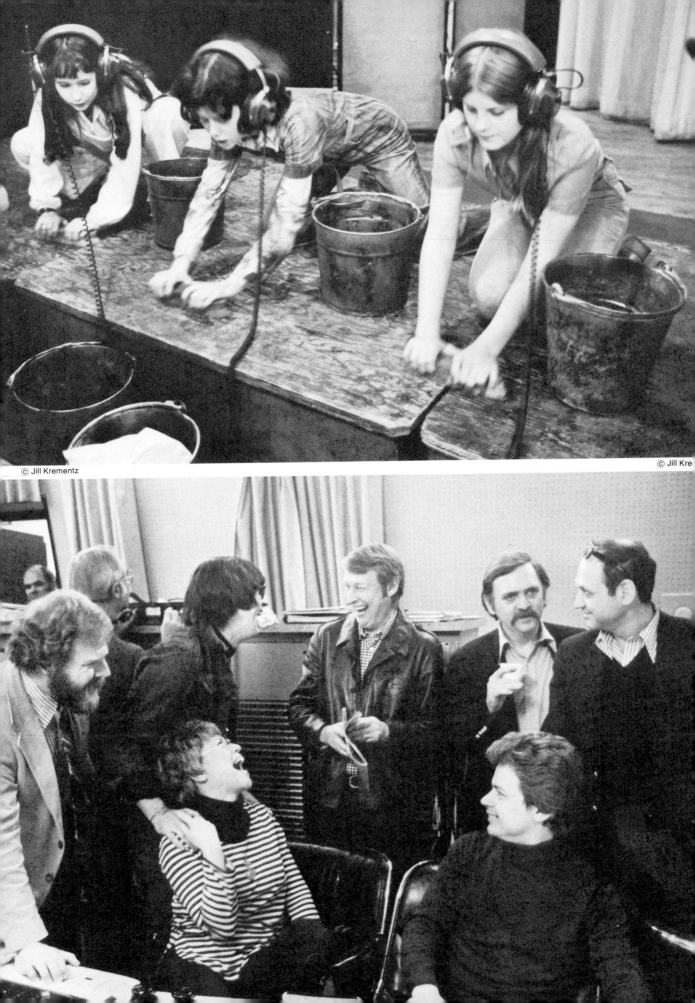

e hope we will be on Broadway for six or seven years. We knew we were going to be at the Alvin for a long time when we discovered that Jimmy Nederlander, the owner of the Alvin, decided to change the electric sign outside of the theatre to ANNIE from ALVIN, which it has been for fifty years.

Bill Yoscary

Bill Yoscary

You have to be very careful about not wearing out your welcome too early. You have problems maintaining the original energy and excitement in a show. The audience now comes in preconditioned, knowing that they are seeing a major hit. Their level of acceptance is doubled, but their level of expectancy is tripled. Once you are a hit, you have to stay a hit.

I often go to the theatre to make sure the actors aren't getting too comfortable in their roles, that they are still giving 100 percent. Sometimes the temptation is to take too much for granted, to feel that you can get away with anything because you're a hit. As director I have to monitor the company on occasion—to be stern and a little bit dictatorial—for my responsibility is to keep the tone and the condition of the show alive at every performance.

The children face a totally different problem. They have been celebrated and applauded. They have gotten more publicity than any group of children I can remember. It's hard for them to maintain a balance because they are still children. In September they returned to school, which helped to restore some normalcy to their lives. During the early part of the run in Washington and New York, they had tutors because they couldn't go to school and do the show at the same time. Now that we can plan in advance when the publicity sessions will be held and what the rehearsal schedules will be, they are enrolled in private schools and attend classes in the morning.

Jill Krementz

They are handling success very well, I think. They still get more excited about going to see *Star Wars* than about the bravos and cheers at the end of the show. They love to play baseball and jacks, to play pinball, and do all kinds of kid things. They loved the fact the *Annie* company had a baseball team during the summer. We

HUH- YUH'D THINK IT WAS CHEATIN' TO STUDY YER LESSONS AROUND HERE- LET 'EM GET SORE- I'M GOIN' TO SCHOOL TO LEARN SOMETHIN-

Reg. U. S. Pat. Off.:
Copyright, 1936, by Chicago
Tribune-N. Y. News Syndicate, Inc.

HAROLD GRAY

Dick Van Dyke

got into the Broadway show league a bit too late, so we were only able to play a few games with some other latecomers. We had one big game with the Bad News Bears, and, alas, got trounced. Our little girls are not seasoned players, but they looked good—even Sandy was outfitted with the team's red and white jacket and cap.

They are professional children now and are making steady, comfortable salaries. But, the kids are still kids, and that's very reassuring. They cry like kids and laugh like kids; they love to skateboard, and they scrape their knees like kids. I have to

Sammy Davis, Jr.

Jacqueline Onassis

scold them as a father now more than as a director because I don't want them to hurt themselves. They are fascinated with the celebrities who come backstage after the show. Dick Van Dyke came backstage in tears; Sammy Davis, Jr. was also in awe of their work; and, before you knew it, the kids were asking them for their autographs.

One of the great joys of *Annie* is the success that Dorothy Loudon has had. She was on Broadway before but was unlucky; perhaps she hadn't had the right material. *Annie* is the first time the role and Dorothy have met head-on and embraced one

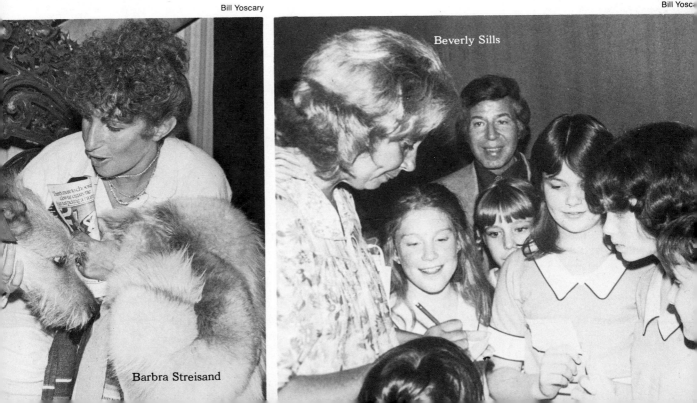

Beverly Sills

Barbra Streisand

Liv Ullmann

Lady Bird Johnson

Hal Linden

Governor
Hugh Carey

Muhammad Ali

Andy Warhol

The New York

Drama Critics' Circle

Award

for the
Best Musical
1976-1977

Annie

BOOK BY *Thomas Meehan* MUSIC BY *Charles Strouse*
LYRICS AND DIRECTION BY *Martin Charnin*
PRODUCED BY *Mike Nichols*
AND *Irwin Meyer, Stephen R. Friedman, Lewis Allen,*
ALVIN NEDERLANDER ASSOCIATES, INC., THE JOHN F. KENNEDY CENTER for the PERFORMING ARTS,
ICARUS PRODUCTIONS, in association with *Peter Crane*
MUSICAL NUMBERS CHOREOGRAPHED BY *Peter Gennaro*

PRESIDENT *Douglas Watt*

another to produce this kind of success and recognition. She won a Tony award for
Best Actress in a Musical—a well-deserved Tony award, after a lifetime of hard
work.

The Tonys are the theatre's highest tribute. They are the equivalent of the
Oscars in the film industry and the Emmys in television. They are the way that the
theatre honors its best each year. We got ten Tony nominations. We could have won
only nine because Dorothy and Andrea were nominated for the same award. *Annie*
won seven awards: Best Costumes, Best Scenic Designer, Best Choreography, Best
Actress in Musical, Best Score and Lyrics of a Musical, Best Book of a Musical, and,
best of all, Best Musical. Charles had won Tony Awards previously for *Applause* and
Bye Bye Birdie, but none of the others had ever won one.

Annie also won the New York Drama Critic's Circle Award as the best musical of
1977, the Outer Critic Circle Award, and many Drama Desk awards. Andrea
McArdle won a Theatre World Award for the most promising new personality on
the Broadway stage.

Sometimes I stand at the back of the house at the curtain calls, and I hear more and more people singing "Tomorrow" along with the company. It's a wonderful moment for me.

I sing along too.

MARTIN CHARNIN celebrated his twentieth year in show business in 1977. He began his career as an actor in the original Broadway production of *West Side Story* in 1957, in which he created the role of Big Deal, performing "Gee, Officer Krupke" over one thousand times on Broadway and on the road. He produced and directed night club acts for Larry Kert, Nancy Wilson, Leslie Uggams, José Ferrer, Dionne Warwick, Mary Travers, among others. He wrote the lyrics for *Hot Spot; Zenda;* collaborated with Richard Rodgers on *Two by Two;* conceived and directed *Nash at Nine,* and with Alan Jay Lerner, a history of the American Musical Theatre, *Music, Music.* He received a gold record for "The Best Thing You've Ever Done," for which he wrote the music and the lyrics for Barbra Streisand. On television, he conceived, produced, directed, and wrote nine specials, among them Anne Bancroft's "Annie: The Women in the Life of a Man," which won him two Emmys; "George M!" and "'S Wonderful, 'S Marvelous," for which he won two more Emmys and the Peabody Award for Broadcasting.

MARTHA SWOPE came to New York to study ballet but soon became interested in photographing dance, theatre, and the arts. Her books include *Martha Graham, Portrait of the Lady as an Artist; The New York City Ballet* by Lincoln Kirstein; and *Baryshnikov at Work.*

BILL YOSCARY works not only as a photographer but backstage as well. Currently he is the house property man for the Alvin Theatre. In addition to photography assignments for magazines and newspapers, he is an accomplished sculptor and has done busts of James Earl Jones, Tammy Grimes, Walter Pigeon, and many more.

JILL KREMENTZ is a well-known photographer of literary figures, a documentary photographer, and an author. A frequent contributor to magazines and other periodicals, she has photographs in the permanent collections in the Museum of Modern Art, the Delaware Art Museum, and the Library of Congress. Her books include *A Very Young Dancer* and *A Very Young Rider.*

NANCY ETHEREDGE, designer of *Annie: A Theatre Memoir,* is a native New Yorker. She received her art training in local schools and on the design staffs of three prestigious New York book publishers. Versatile and prolific, her work ranges from childrens books to medical textbooks, and she is the holder of numerous awards and citations.